TALES FROM

A

WEE

SCOTTISH

VILLAGE

by

Karen McGarr

PROLOGUE

With tears streaming down her cheeks faster than she can wipe them away, mum waves frantically as the coach reverses slowly out of the bay in Buchanan Station. Huddled together against the cold and smirr Scotland is known for, the small cluster of family and friends that have come to see us off wave and blow kisses until their silhouettes become blurry.

As the coach sharply rounds the bend I catch a quick glimpse of dad in the seat behind. His smile, that I usually find reassuring, does nothing to calm the somersault my stomach does when I think about the new school I'll be starting on Monday.

Reaching between the seats, dad lightly squeezes mum's shoulder.

"Y'awright Lizzie?"

"Aye," she sniffs, patting his hand. "I'll be fine when we get there."

"Only seven hours to go-o," he says in a sing-song voice. "You ok, hen?"

"Uh-huh," I fib, fixing my gaze on the dog-eared copy of *84 Charing Cross Road* that my English teacher pressed into my palm the day before, long after the prefects had given up on any hope of an orderly exit.

"I've read it more times than I care to admit," Mrs. McAlpine had uttered in her broad Doric dialect. "And if truth be told, I doubt I'll ever make it as far as London, but it cheers me to think there might *still* be wee bookshops, just like it."

With more than a slight blush, she added, "Owned by a man like Frank."

I didn't have the heart to tell her the town we were moving to was sixty miles outside of London, created purely to aid with a post war housing shortage.

Built on existing farmland, Milton Keynes, in the county of Buckinghamshire, boasted of a grid road system comparable to that of New York. Pamphlets provided by the Milton Keynes Development Corporation stated no building would be taller than the tallest tree, while accompanying literature displayed glossy pictures of houses of every description.

Two months prior, dad showed up for his shift at the car plant in Linwood, where, a few years before, he'd narrowly missed losing a finger whilst working on the assembly line that churned out Hillman Imps.

After clocking in alongside the men he'd come to know during his dozen years of employment, word spread across the factory floor that the doors would be shutting that day. For good. Rather than delay getting caught up in the mass exodus, dad took his leave and made his way back to the bus stop.

From his seat on the top deck, he gasped when he saw the line of men snaked around the Glasgow building that housed the job centre. With the imminent addition of several thousand more about to lose their livelihood in the declining 1981 economy, he stayed on the bus.

From across the dinner table dad looked like he had the weight of the world on his shoulders and, for the first time in my life, I got sent to bed. When I heard the creak of the kitchen door being shut, I sensed serious change was afoot.

The very next day mum and I stood on the platform at Glasgow Central, waving to dad as the train groaned its way out of the station. Many moons before, dad's lifelong friend had moved down south. Now, married with two daughters, Harry and his family were enjoying life in the place dad described in his letters as, *booming*.

Within a couple of weeks, dad secured a job with a new home improvement company and with each phone call he sounded chirpier, excited at the prospect of the three of us being together again.

"Ye won't believe this place," he gushed. "There's new hooses sprouting up everywhere."

One of those houses, an end of terrace with three bedrooms and, *a garden the size of a fitba pitch* was to become ours. Hours were spent on the phone discussing what mum coined *The English Move*, a phrase she tutted with an extra dose of disdain. Whenever she'd hang up from talking to dad, she'd roll her eyes and ask me to help her pack. After allowing *me* to choose what *I* wanted to take, invariably she'd say there was something she had to tell her sister/mother/cousin/niece/friend. The closer it got to moving day, the longer mum spent on the phone with her closest kin, most of whom had never lived more than a few miles from where they were born.

True to my fourteen-year old self, I soon become bored with the Victorian architecture, my interest piqued only by the sight of the landmarks I've come to know from recent jaunts to the city centre with my best friend Linda, who I've promised to write to at least once a week.

I bury my head in the pages of Frank and Helen's contrasting worlds and quickly lose myself in their transatlantic love affair. By the time the winter light fades, mum is out for the count, the top of her head pressed against my shoulder, her chest slowly rising and falling in a way I don't wish to disturb by reaching up to turn on the light.

My drooping eyelids give in to the lull of the engine and I drift off into a nightmarish scenario, where I show up at my new school wearing my old school uniform. Waking with a start, relieved that it was only a dream, I look out at the pyres dotted across the flat English landscape.

"Guy Fawkes," I mouth, reclaiming my arm. The jerky movement stirs mum awake.

"Would ye look at that!" she exclaims, her eyes widening at the sight of the flickering flames reaching as far as the eye can see.

When dad pops his head between the seats and hisses, "Boo!" mum and I scream the same piercing sound that causes the woman seated a few rows in front to shake her permed hair and cluck disapprovingly. Stifling a giggle, I slump into the seat while mum cranes her neck in dad's direction.

"I thought they only had bonfires in London."

"Apparently not," he responds, his Glaswegian accent giving the first word four syllables. "Hopefully the new hoose'll still be standing!"

Mum looks at me. "Did *you* know aboot this?"

"Why of course, mama," I frown, with my best attempt at received pronunciation. "The legend of that dastardly man, Fawkes, traversed from the sooty chimney stacks of Londinium *all the way* to the craggy hills of Caledonia."

"Haud yer wheest, missy," she says, with a playful swipe to my leg. "Yer no too big to get leathered."

A few minutes later, mum draws a heavy sigh that prompts me to ask her if she's ok.

"Aye, it's just..." Her voice trails off and she dabs at her eyes.

Dad's handkerchief appears between the seats. "We'll be fine, Lizzie. Come and sit with me."

Signs for Milton Keynes begin to appear and my stomach churns with a mixture of excitement and dread. I can't wait to see the new house and pick out my bedroom but I'm fretting about my bike, hoping it'll arrive intact and in time to get me to school on Monday.

Shortly after exiting the motorway, the driver navigates an endless number of roundabouts.

"These bloody things are making me dizzy," mum says, her head lolling from side-to-side like something out of a cartoon.

Ignoring the freshly painted white lines, the driver parks in one of the dozen or so empty bays and with the engine hissing our arrival, we disembark, leaving three passengers remaining on the coach, for the last leg of the journey to London.

Posters with no trace of tattered edges show smiling children in park-like settings, holding red balloons.

"Looks like the rag man's been," mum mutters under her breath, her eyes glinting with mischief. On the concourse, a vending machine illuminates a corner of the otherwise stark, grey building. "Go and get me a wee Irn Bru, hen," she pleads.

"Good luck finding that doon here, missus," the driver remarks, as he passes on his way to the toilet.

Slouching in front of a row of metal benches offering zero comfort against the November chill, my ears prick up when a cabbie with a cockney accent so authentic it sounds fake, asks, "Where to guv?"

Speaking much slower than usual, dad gives him the address. Eyeing the excess amount of luggage, the cabbie cocks his head. "You coming 'ere to live?"

Dad nods his response and the cabbie slaps his meaty palm against the shoulder of dad's corduroy jacket. "Good on ya, mate!"

Reaching for the biggest suitcase, the cabbie glances in my direction.

"This one yours, treacle? I've a bricks and mortar about your age, can't keep up with all that Top of the Pops stuff she blasts up the apples and pears." He looks at mum. "Me trouble and strife says I spoil 'er." He shrugs in dad's direction. "That's women mate, innit?"

Two roundabouts later, the cabbie points to a mirrored glass structure, the likes of which I've only ever seen on the tv show, Dallas. "That there, my friends, is the new John Wayne station. There's a rumour," he taps a finger to his nose, "that the 'ole baked bean 'erself will be cutting the ribbon."

In nothing resembling a whisper, mum says, "Whit's he saying?"

I catch the cabbie's wink in the rearview mirror as mum nudges closer to me.

"D'ye think everybody here will speak like *that*?"

"Nah, luv," the cabbie chirps. "Just the ole muckers like me, from lun dun."

Mum looks at me expectantly.

"He said everybody here speaks like that."

"Och, you two," dad chuckles, as the cabbie pulls up outside the house my parents will call home for the next seventeen years.

NEWS OF THE MOVE

You're doing what?"

"We're going home!" dad's voice booms from three thousand miles away.

"Isn't England home?"

"Scotland will *always* be home," he proclaims, my brain swiftly conjuring up images of him standing at the edge of John O'Groats, his fist pumping the air. "Don't get me wrong," he continues, "life in England has been good to us, but it's time for a wee change."

"Dad, I'd hardly consider moving four hundred miles a *wee* change."

"Uff, we did it before and we'll do it again!" I smile in response to his can-do attitude but my mind is already in overdrive at what such a move means.

To me.

"I never expected you'd leave, especially after all the work you've done to the house, not to mention your friends-"

And of course mine!

"Och, they can come and visit but they won't be able to stay for long."

"Why is that?"

"The cottage is tiny."

"The... cottage?" I stutter, feeling a knot quickly knitting my eyebrows together. With my eyes closed, I see dad standing in the hall, phone in hand. There's only ever been one phone, a rotary phone, which, after I got married and moved to America, garnered many a joke about how long it took to dial my number.

The phone has always taken pride of place on the shelf dad crafted from an old side table that barely survived the move to England. Underneath the phone sits a Yellow Pages, more commonly referred to by mum as "The big phone book." Next to the phone sits "The wee phone book," bursting at the seams with the names and telephone numbers of everyone she's ever known, alongside which she scribbled a few words on how they became acquainted. The first page alone references entries such as; Married her brother, Chip Shop, Karen's school pal, Tom's terrible boss.

"The phone chair," a green leather Chesterfield, dominates the narrow hallway, leaving me to wonder why my parents didn't replace it with something more fitting. The spot of many an hour spent on the phone, my aching from growing pains legs draped over the side, my hand covering the mouthpiece, whispering to my friends, mostly about boys, while mum, all ears and excuses, passed in and out of the hall.

On the other side of the pond, cordless phone in hand, I plop into the wingback chair I paid peanuts for in a thrift store. During one of dad's visits, while I was hosting an open house with the hope of selling it, he replaced the outdated velour with a blue and white check tablecloth I no longer used.

Long past the age of dangling legs, I make a poor attempt at getting comfortable in a chair designed for nothing other than sitting ramrod straight.

"Aye, the wee cottage," dad continues. "That's the reason I'm phoning, I wanted to share the good news with ye."

I was so stunned I couldn't speak.

"It's a wee gem," he gushed. "Well, it will be after we replace, och, pretty much everything!"

I shoot up out of the chair. "You bought a cottage? In Scotland?" He ignores my churlish tone, promptly answering the question I didn't get the chance to ask.

"It's in Ayrshire."

"Ayrshire," I mouth, tracing the tip of my index finger on an imaginary map of Scotland.

Dad comes from a family of fifteen, five of whom didn't survive infancy. When he was a toddler, his sixteen-year old sister Dorothy died from Tuberculosis. Two years later, his nineteen year-old sister Betty also succumbed, leaving my Grandparents with eight of the fifteen children my Granny bore.

The family lived on the ground floor of a tenement in Dennistoun with barely enough space for half of them. The toilet was outside. Fortunately, my Grandfather possessed not only the gift of the gab but also a green thumb that enabled him to grow much of their food in a small patch of garden. Dad often recalled the hardships he endured growing up and, like many families, the sibling dynamics that played out, more so in such cramped quarters.

Dad was baby number thirteen, after which my Granny gave birth to a third set of twins. Partly due to the ten-year gap in age, dad and Patrick weren't especially close, which is why I was surprised when, the week before, dad told me he was going to visit Patrick.

"He'll be back in no time," mum uttered, a clear absence of faith in any brotherly bond.

Dad accompanied his brother to view a farmhouse he was interested in buying. As it turned out, the barren property came with too hefty a price tag but on their way out of the village, they passed a cottage that piqued dad's interest and he asked Patrick to stop the car. Patrick ignored his younger brother's request and kept driving. Dad asked again, this time with the addition of a few choice words

"It sits on the banks of the River Ayr," dad continues.

"Sounds idyllic," I say, racking my brain for long forgotten images of bonnie banks and bracken hills.

"The river runs under the auld brig, built back in the day, after one of the parishioners drowned when he was fording the river on his way to church."

I shudder at the thought, feasting my eyes on my modern kitchen, marveling at the gleaming counter tops and oversized stainless-steel appliances.

"What does mum have to say about it?"

"She's no seen it yet." His tone is matter of fact, unlike, I expect, mum's reaction when her deranged husband told her what he'd done. "But I know she'll love it."

I hope for your sake you're right!

"We'll be able to sit by the river and if mum wants, we can fish for salmon in season."

I don't dare remind him mum is as far removed from fishing as he appears to be from reality, so I keep my mouth shut.

"There's an abundance of pheasant in the area. Apparently, folk come from all over for shooting parties, not that I agree-"

Fishing and shooting!

"Dad," I say, as calmly as I can muster. "Are you ok? I mean… your health…. is everything alright?"

Or have you totally lost it?

"Couldn't be better," he chirps. "Anyway, I better get a move on, mum's away out shopping and I told her I'd have the kitchen stuff packed and the place all spick and span by the time she gets back."

My response is a heavy eye roll, which considering I'm on the phone, is pointless. "Aren't you getting ahead of yourself, dad? I mean, if the housing market there is anything like it is here, it'll be ages before-"

"Done and dusted," he states.

Flummoxed by the expression I stutter, "You… you already soooold the house?"

"Aye, Michael, you remember Michael I work with, he and his wife are buying it. They've two lads, smashing wee souls, one dark, the other fair, funny how that happens isn't it? The wee yins love the garden and Michael and his wife Aila, she's Finnish, lovely lassie

5

but pale as a ghost, they're already talking about where to put the swing set."

"Oh," I utter, an unexpected combination of anger and sadness catching in my throat.

"Aye!" He exclaims. "When it's time to go, it's time to go!"

Hold on a minute! You sold the home where I spent my teens and beyond? The place where I pored over homework when all I wanted to do was go out with my friends. The home where the three of us would stay up into the early hours putting the world to rights. The place where everyone gathered and lingered in the garden, long after the sun went down. The place where we sang Christmas carols with my now deceased grandparents. The place of a thousand stolen kisses with the first boy I loved.

Still reeling, I know I need to go there one last time, if only to snap a thousand pictures of my toddler son, playing in the garden with the dog, surrounded by my parents and longtime friends

"So," I croak. "When's the big move?"

"We leave in a fortnight."

FIRST IMPRESSIONS

Landing at Glasgow's Abbotsinch Airport for the first time in decades fills me with childhood memories of the first time I flew. I vividly remember how huge the terminal looked and how the butterflies in my tummy fluttered when I climbed up the metal stairs towards the plane. That first flight was to the island of Mallorca, with mum and nana (it'd be a long time before dad would overcome his fear of flying). The hotel had not one, but three swimming pools, my then four-year old idea of heaven.

For the first eight years of my life, we lived on the third floor of a Glasgow tenement. The flat had two rooms and an outside toilet, shared by a family of four who lived across the landing. It astounds me to recall the parties my parents hosted, often with upwards of two dozen people, especially on Hogmanay, dad's favourite night of the year, when we'd link arms after the bells and he'd lead us in, "Auld Lang Syne."

Thanks to countless trips to the, "Swimming baths," I learned to swim at a young age. Dad was the one who taught me how to swim in the public swimming pool we frequented several times a week, mainly to use the showers that seemed luxurious, when the only inside plumbing we had was the kitchen sink!

Stifling a yawn, I marvel at the energy of my toddler son as his blond head bobs around the baggage carousel, loving his gleeful expression when the alarm sounds and the light flashes, indicating the belt is about to kick into action. With his arms open wide, Will comes tottering in my direction. I scoop him up and bounce him on my hip.

"Who are we going to see?"

"Nana."

"Who else?"

"Ganda."

"That's right," I say, switching hips. "We've come to visit nana and granda."

A woman with a kindly face pushes a trolley in my direction. "I remember those days well," she says, in solidarity. Spotting my oversized suitcase with the airline's bright orange "heavy" label attached to the handle, I nod my thanks.

"What a beautiful wee boy, what's his name?"

"William," I say, as he shimmies out of my arms. "This is his first time in Scotland."

The woman steadies the trolley while I sling the suitcase onto it, then I pick up Will and plop him on top of the suitcase.

"Looks like a long stay," she laughs. "I hope the weather's not too dreich while you're here."

"My dad's fond of saying he enjoys Scotland's nine months of rain and three months of bad weather."

"Wise man," she laughs.

Will bounces on top of the suitcase. "Go for ride?"

Through the glass doors that lead into the terminal, I see dad pacing up and down, a newspaper tucked under his arm. Mum's sitting on a bench with her legs crossed, one foot swinging up and down as she tips her head back, draining the remains of a can of Irn Bru.

The double doors glide open and dad is first to spot us. He says something to mum that makes her face light up and gives her a hand up.

"Look," I say, pointing to my beaming parents, guiding Will as he wriggles free. He toddles in their direction and I slowly push the trolley, savouring the sight of the reunion of my parents and their only grandchild.

Squished between my parents, tiny tufts of Will's feathery hair poke out as they shower him in kisses and cuddles. Dad is first to break free, all smiles as he heads in my direction.

"Hiya hen, yer looking well," he says, wrapping me in a hug, planting a kiss on my cheek. "The wee yin's full of beans, how was he on the flight?"

"Good as gold, he slept for most of it."

Mum squeezes me tight and there are lots of oohs and ahhs over how much Will has grown, peppered with questions about the journey.

"What's that?" I ask, eyeing a plush green toy in Will's hand.

"It's the Loch Ness monster," mum says. "When you press the hump, it plays Scotland the Brave."

A new acquaintance of my parents is waiting for us in the car park. We shake hands and I can tell from the inflection of his voice he's asking a question but I haven't a clue what he's saying. I turn my attention to Will, securing him in the car seat dad bought the same day I purchased the airline tickets. Dad teases me about the weight of the suitcase and mum and I pile into the back seat of the estate car.

Once we're out of the city, the buildings shrink and the road opens up to the expansive countryside. I stretch my arm out the window and roll my wrist against the crisp June air.

"This heatwave's no supposed to last," mum says, "but we'll take it while we can, right Fergus?"

Fergus responds with something that sounds like metal being crushed and my parents chuckle. Mum give me a *what's up with you?* look. I shrug my shoulders and motion to Fergus.

"Och Fergus," mum says. "Karen disnae understand yer broad Ayrshire accent."

Fergus adds glass to the crushed metal and I give mum a blank stare.

"He said you'll be fluent by the time ye go back to America."

The road stretches before us and the low trimmed hedgerow affords endless views of green quilted fields, dotted with sheep. Huge marshmallow clouds sail slowly in the pale blue sky, making me wish I could paint. Dad turns around and pulls a funny face that makes Will chuckle. "We're nearly there."

A few minutes later, I follow mum's finger as she points to a commanding sandstone structure with an arched opening, leading to what appears to be a never-ending tree lined driveway.

"That's the gatehouse to the castle," she beams.

"Yeah, right," I smirk. "And I'm Rapunzel."

The sound of laughter bounces around the car and Will gleefully kicks his Toy Story sneakers.

Bursts of moss dot the stone wall running along the steep incline leading to the sign bearing the name of the village. Beyond the wall, verdant ferns sway, greedily vying for droplets of water cascading down from narrow waterfalls that join streams with a sound so soothing, I open the window all the way.

Once on level ground, the church comes into view and I utter, "How lovely," to no-one in particular.

"Sixteen fifty-eight," dad states proudly, as though he built it with his own bare hands.

I'm still basking in the beauty of the church when the car comes to a screeching halt, propelling us forward. Instinctively, my hand shoots across mum to Will but her hand is already firmly on him. Growling an expression that I have no difficulty understanding, Fergus jerks open the car door and jumps out, then he pokes his head back in. "Sorry!"

"Baaaaa," Will babbles, pointing to a dozen or so sheep spread across the road.

Dad gets out of the car. "This'll be Duncan's lot," he tuts, as he and Fergus work in tandem in an attempt to move the sheep off the road.

My gaze is back on the church when mum nudges me impatiently. "I said we can get oot. That's us here," she says motioning to the other side of the street, where a stone cottage, festooned with basket upon basket of tumbling flowers sits. Adjacent to the cottage on the right sits a low-level bridge, with an opening that looks wide enough for nothing bigger than a wheelbarrow.

"Is that really it?"

"Aye," she states, practically pushing me out of the car.

Will wriggles with excitement as I release the safety harness and Fergus wastes no time slipping back behind the wheel, drumming his fingers impatiently while he waits for dad to move enough sheep for the car to get through.

"Take mummy's hand," mum says, as Fergus zooms off. "Ye need to keep yer wits aboot ye on this wee bend, cars sometimes come flying and the last thing we need is a pile of slaughtered sheep!"

With that grisly visual, I grab Will and follow dad's lead as he continues shooing the sheep from the road, onto the grassy knoll.

"Liz, can you go and phone Duncan?"

I'm about to ask who Duncan is but with a heavy eyeroll, mum beats me to it. "The shepherd."

There's something about dad's handling of the sheep I find amusing, maybe because I've always considered him as more of a city dweller than a country squire.

"Get you, dad! You'll be buying a Collie dog next."

With a grin, he continues banding the sheep together.

"This is the third time this week we've had to track Duncan down. I don't know where the break in the fence is but the sooner he fixes it, the better."

"Sweep," Will coos.

"Dad, is it ok if Will touches them?"

He shoots me *a look*.

I raise my hands in defense. "There's no sheep on Cape Cod!"

From outside the front door, mum hollers, "Tom! Lottie said Duncan's in the pub."

Dad nods in acknowledgement. "That's where Fergus thought he'd be. Wait here a wee minute."

"With the sheep?"

"Keep them out of harm's way!" he shouts over his shoulder as he makes his way to the cottage.

"But, dad…"

No sooner is he out of sight when the sheep begin to separate.

"Shi- " I begin, quickly catching myself. I zig-zag behind them, shouting, "Shoo," but my voice falters and the death cursed sheep start ambling towards the road. My arm is aching from the weight of Will, so I put him down. "Come and help mummy!"

"Shew!" He shrieks in the demonic voice young children adopt when they're overtired or extremely excited. "Shew! Shew! Shew!"

With my pint-sized helper in tow, I manage to keep the sheep at a safe distance from the road but I still sigh with relief when I spot dad coming out of the cottage. In his hand, he carries a bright orange sign, emblazoned with; CAUTION! SHEEP! leaving me to wonder where on earth he found such a thing. Appraising the bucolic scene before him, he shouts, "Nice work, little bo- peep!"

"I may have been up all night," I boast mockingly. "But my herding skills are clearly still intact!"

Dad motions to the car as Fergus slowly pulls into the layby. Next to him sits a young man wearing a baseball cap.

"That's the shepherd?"

Dad nods. "Aye and depending on how much Duncan has had to drink, we might have to give him a wee hand getting the sheep back up the hill and into the field."

"No way," I groan. "I'm fit for nothing but a cup of tea."

Dad nods towards the cottage. "I hope you're hungry, mum's prepared enough food to feed-"

"An entire flock?" I laugh.

Heeding mum's warning about the over-zealous drivers, I gather up Will and he chuckles when I mimic the way he squints his eyes against the rays splitting through the hawthorn trees. On the other side of the road, black wrought iron railings sit atop the stone wall surrounding the church and cemetery. Moss covered ancient headstones tilt forward, while others crumble closer to the earth.

Up close, the cottage evokes memories of the fairy-tales my nana read to me from the library book I signed out again and again. Underneath each of the two windows, vibrant blooms spill from wooden boxes painted fire engine red. A small porch supported by timber frames covers the front door, attached to which is a brass door knocker in the shape of a lion's head. The sight of the brass letter box produces pangs of nostalgia with memories of what felt like eons, waiting for letters from my then fiancé. Reaching up, I run my hand over the painted sign bearing the name of the cottage, pausing to inhale the heady scent of jasmine.

"Go see nana?" Will pushes the front door all the way open and I call inside to make sure mum is there.

"Send him through!" she yells from somewhere in the back of the cottage.

The entry hallway is tiny and the door to the left is ajar. I step into the small bedroom and with the light streaming in, the room radiates comfort and warmth. I run my fingers over the gilt winged angel that's graced mum's bedside table for as long as I can remember. A wave of weariness washes over me as I gaze longingly at the white lace trimmed pillowcases piled high on the bed.

The other door leads to the living room, the focal point of which is a huge fireplace with a tall stone mantle adorned with pictures, candlesticks and a small crystal vase with yellow roses. Taking pride of place in the centre of the mantle is a gold carriage clock that belonged to my paternal grandparents, next to which sits a little copper plaque with mum's favourite saying; "Give thanks with a grateful heart."

Will comes running into the room, squealing, "Boon!" while Mum trails behind, an array of colourful balloons blocking her face. "Balloons for ma wee darlin," she coos. "Och, there you are!" she says, stopping in her tracks. "Would you like the grand tour, m'lady," she jokes, releasing the balloons to take my arm.

I've been in the real estate business for years but mum feels the need to point out that the room we're standing in is the living room. Will bats at the balloons as I comment on the grandness of the fireplace.

"We used it last week for the first time and almost burned the place to a cinder! Some poor wee animal made its way in but obviously no oot." She shudders. "The smoke was so bad, dad had to phone the fire brigade. Then he had to paint the ceiling. Again!"

"Is this where the ceiling collapsed?"

"Aye, the stour was everywhere. I'm still hoovering up wee bits of plaster."

"You'd never know this place was in such disrepair. If I didn't know better I'd say you'd been here for years."

"Dad's been going gangbusters."

"As have you, mum, by the looks of it."

We move into the bedroom, where the pillows once again beckon and the fireplace I failed to notice the first time screams, "cosy." A row of fitted floor to ceiling wardrobes line the back wall.

I hear dad whistle and look out the window to see him coming through the gate. The church bell catches my eye and I make a mental note to be up in time to hear and watch it on Sunday.

"That's them safely back in the field," dad says, brushing his hands. "That Duncan's a character, nothing ever seems to bother him."

"That's because he's always hauf cut," mum chirps. "He spends more time in the pub that he does in the fields."

"C'mon wee man," dad says, picking up Will, the balloon string still in his pudgy fist.

"I'll take ye down to the river and show ye how to skip stones."

Mum brushes wisps of hair off Will's forehead. "He's probably tired, Tom." She plants a kiss on Will's cheek that he promptly wipes away with the back of his hand.

Dad swats at the balloon. "Yer no tired, are you Will?"

Will shakes his head furiously, flashing his toothy grin.

"Of course yer no tired! Yer half Scottish!" dad bellows, the vibration of which lingers after he leaves the room.

I perch on the edge of the bed and mum opens the wardrobe door to an abundance of colourful long and short sleeved dresses and tops, hanging in a way she calls *higgledy piggledy*. Inwardly, I smile at the thought of my closet three thousand miles away, where everything has its place and the hangers all face the same way. From a

17

shelf piled high with shoes and bags, she retrieves a small box and hands it to me.

"There's a few wee bits and pieces in there that belonged to nana. It's no much but I thought you'd want to have them."

My nana has been dead for eight years, but at the mention of her name, my eyes brim with tears.

With her eyes downcast, mum says, "You don't have to open it now."

"Thanks, mum," I say, running my fingers over the blue velvet lid. "I still really miss her, I know you do too."

"Aye, she was a good wee soul," she says, reaching out her hand to pull me up off the bed.

The kitchen and bathroom are housed in an addition at the back of the cottage. In the bathroom, mum unscrews tube after tube of lotions she shoves under my nose, urging me, in the worst French accent ever, to, "Smell zis." With her hand on the door knob to what can only be the kitchen, she purrs, "And now, Mademoiselle! The piece de insistence!"

"Resistance!" I laugh, shaking my head.

"Oui oui," she says throatily, opening the door with a flourish.

The double arches of the bridge dominate the view in the oversized window that runs the length of the sink and the draining board. With the side door open, the sound of the river babbling its way under the arches fills the air with a sense of calm.

"Unbelievable," I say, gripping the edge of the sink for support as I rise on my tip toes and look out the window, down below to where dad and Will are at the water's edge. Resting on his haunches, dad puts a pebble in Will's hand. I tap on the window and when dad looks up, he raises his finger, gesturing, "Wait." He guides Will's hand as he tosses the pebble. It plops on the surface, not far from Will's bare feet but dad claps and Will holds out his hand for another. Dad points up to the window and Will looks up and gives a distracted wave. I give him a thumbs up and step back from the sink.

"Looks like a painting," I breathe, pausing to take in the view with mum by my side.

"That view is the only reason I never throttled your Father the night we arrived."

"Lucky for him they'd just finished constructing it!" Mum smiles at my poor joke, pulls out a chair and motions for me to sit. She reaches over me to put the teapot on the table and the light catches her sparkly earring, inducing memories of my teens.

Lengthy bouts of depression plagued mum for much of her life. Winter was always when it'd rear its ugly head, making Christmas especially difficult. Mum's episodes with what she called, "the dark tunnel," would last for months, some of which would be spent in a psychiatric setting.

Sometimes, she'd come home while I was still at school. Before I had a chance to open the gate to store my bike in the garden shed, I'd hear her belting out a Connie Francis song. The smell of something hearty would come wafting through the kitchen window and I'd poke my head in, noticing her freshly washed hair, lips shiny with pale pink lipstick and sparkly drop earrings.

Swaying in time to the music, she looked nothing like the heavily medicated woman I never really got to know.

"You must be shattered," she says, adding a generous amount of milk to make the tea a perfect tone. Greedily, I gulp it down in one.

"Ah, Scottish water," I sigh contentedly. "Makes the best tea in the world."

"I've square sausages, eggs and tattie scones but I thought you might want one of these first." She pushes a plate of strawberry tarts in my direction. I pick one up and raise it like a trophy.

"I don't remember the last time I had one of these." I take a blissful bite, causing the pastry to crumble, so I stuff the remainder in my mouth.

The sound of dad and Will approaching drifts through the side door and mum gives me a knowing smile. Reaching across the table, she squeezes my hand.

"Welcome home, hen."

THE ENFORCER

Mum's phone calls are sporadic but dad and I have a standing order every Wednesday, "At three my time," during which he relays the latest in a long string of anecdotes I call "Talky Tommy's." This one beginning with, "The door went at tea time." If you were raised anywhere other than Scotland, you might be more inclined to say something along the lines of, "The doorbell rang during dinner."

Dad opens the door to a small statured man who introduces himself as, "Trevor Bastion Churchill. Enforcement Officer with the BBC."

Dad invites him in.

"I'd rather not," the stranger mumbles, shuffling nervously. "You can't imagine how many times I've been assaulted!"

I envision mum scurrying around the kitchen, stashing plates of uneaten food in the microwave. I'm sure she's also filling the tea kettle to the brim, pondering what biscuits she has to offer the dinner hour intruder.

If you're not from the UK, you might be wondering what on earth Mr. Bastion-Churchill actually does. As mentioned, he's an "Enforcement Officer," which has nothing to do with the military. An Enforcement Officer has the daunting task of visiting people the British Broadcasting Company believe to have broken the law by failing to purchase a television licence. Yes, a licence to watch television.

Introduced on June 1st, 1946, the licence covered the monochrome-only single channel. The licence at that time cost two pounds. In January 1968 a "Colour Supplement" of five pounds was added.

Today, after decades of period dramas and documentaries free from advertisements, the licence will set you back £157.50

Should you require a licence for a black and white television, the cost is £53.

If you're registered as blind, the licence can be obtained for half price (?!) and if you're over the age of 75, they let you have it for free.

Given the fact Mr. Bastion-Churchill is an Englishman with the audacity to show up during the Scotsman's evening meal, flaunting his double-barreled name no less, dad deviously opens the door all the way. "Come in! Come in! I promise I won't harm ye!" Displaying a great deal of trepidation, the enforcer crosses the threshold into the Scotsman's lair.

Perched on the edge of the couch with his ankles touching, Mr. Bastion-Churchill happily accepts mum's overzealous offer of tea, before, "Making a big show," of clicking open his briefcase, which dad describes as "A very un ness a sery prop."

Shuffling through a stack of papers, he tuts, "Licence evasion," just loud enough for dad to hear. Coming up short, Mr. Bastion-Churchill snaps the briefcase shut but keeps it on his lap. After, "A very theatrical sigh," he begins to explain the reason for his visit.

With his hands clasped on top of the briefcase, The Enforcer informs dad that from inside the detection van he and his associate were able to tell that the unlicensed television was set to standby. "The technology has become so advanced that the room in which said *culprit*." He cackles at his choice of word. "Also known as *the television*, can be detected from sixty metres away."

Dad eyes the oversized wooden cabinet in the corner of the room that houses the television. "Is that so, Mr. Bastion Churchill?"

"Please, call me Trevor" he gushes, blowing on the tea mum served, not in an everyday mug but in a china cup and saucer. With a newfound confidence now that he feels his safety is no longer in peril, he looks directly at dad.

"My boss is stark raving mad at the nerve of you!" Dad raises his eyebrows in question.

"We know that just a week ago, whilst still *not* in possession of a license, you had the *audacity* to go out and purchase a *new* television."

When you buy a television in the UK, your information is entered into a database system known as LASSY. The database is routinely updated with licence details and anyone buying or renting a television will be identified in this system, which in turn means you will need a licence to watch your new television. TV Licensing maintains records of every address in the database that is recorded as not being in possession of a tv licence, the cottage clearly being one of them.

In the past, BBC Enforcement Officers would patrol the streets in vans that were easily recognizable from their huge antennas and lettering but now, they're white unmarked vans with all of the technology tucked safely inside. Equipment that includes hand-held devices access even closer reads on where the unlicensed tv's are situated inside a home!

Sipping delicately at the sugary tea, Mr. Bastion Churchill informs dad the next step will be a date to appear in court. "You can be fined up to one thousand pounds you know," he states confidently. "Plus, of course, the price of a licence."

"Is that right?" Dad's expression is delivered as more of an acknowledgement than a question. At this point, I imagine mum eavesdropping from the other side of the living room door, hushing the dog whilst making a mental note to throttle dad for failing to, *"Do the right thing!"*

"However," Trevor continues smugly. "You can save yourself from all of that *inconvenience* by purchasing a tv licence. Right now, in fact. From moi!"

Suppressing a grin, dad reaches for the brass handle on what Mum calls, "The wee cubby beside the settee," and with the enforcer's beady eyes on him, removes a manila folder. Painstakingly, dad opens the folder, each precise movement forcing Mr. BC to lean forward, so much so, that he topples off the couch!

Dad averts his eyes while he waits for the enforcer to reclaim his spot, then, "With a great deal of flourish," hands him a crisp copy of a valid British Broadcasting Company Television Licence.

Mr. Bastion-Churchill pushes his glasses up from the bridge of his nose and scans the licence.

"Ye'd have thought he was looking for the Da Vinci Code!"

"Aha!" he exclaims, jabbing his finger on the licence.

"Pray tell," dad utters, for the first time in his life.

"The postcode. *Your* postcode." His voice rises in excitement. "The name of the cottage is the same but the postcode doesn't match. See?" Standing, he passes the licence to dad with a smug expression.

"Seems you're off the hook Mr. McGarr. Although I must say, you didn't strike me as the sort to, as one would say, *dodge the system*, but one never can tell!"

"Poor Trevor," I say. "That must surely be one of the worst jobs ever. I feel sorry for him."

"Och, so did I."

"Doesn't sound like it! I bet he couldn't wait to leave."

"I wouldnae be so sure about that."

"Please don't tell me you continued to torture the poor man."

"Just a wee bit," dad chuckles. "I couldnae help it."

25

"Pray tell, Thomas," I clip in my crustiest upper-class voice.

"I offered him a wee dram."

"What's bad about that?"

"It was the cheap stuff. The kind that burns the back of your throat."

BUS FARE

Unlike mum, dad has always been an early riser. Every morning after walking the dog, he makes a mug of *the too strong for me* tea he enjoys, perched on the small wall right outside the kitchen door, hoping for a glimpse of the grey heron or maybe even an otter or two.

Still jetlagged from my arrival the day before, I stumble outside, tugging the belt on mum's terry cloth robe tightly around my waist.

"Summer in Scotland," dad jokes. "Tea?"

"I'll get it," I yawn, a sliver of cold pulsing through me. "You ready for a top-up?"

"Aye." Dad passes the empty mug. "No too much milk and keep the teabags for the compost bin. Stick mum's baffies on, yer no on the beaches of Cape Cod."

Pointing to his feet, I say, "What are *those*?"

"Socks."

"*Tartan* socks?"

"Aye," he grins. "They issue them at the border between England and Scotland."

I roll my eyes and step inside, where the temperature is less than that of outside. I click the tea kettle on and dad motions to mum's fluffy purple slippers, strewn underneath the kitchen table. While I'm squashing my feet into them, dad says, "You'll find hats and mittens on the shelf behind the kitchen door."

Mittens!

With a mug of piping hot tea in my mitten free hands and a wool hat emblazoned with *Glasgow Smiles Better* pulled down over my ears, I say, "I thought the slogan was Glasgow's Miles Better?"

"T'is," dad nods. "Mum's wee pal, Jeanette got mixed up when she embroidered it."

In satisfied tones, dad points out the abundance of bushes and flowers he planted back when the cottage windows were still boarded up, in other words, as soon as they moved in.

With a sense of ease that I can't imagine ever adopting, the Latin names roll off his tongue. "That's Devils-bit scabious, part of the honeysuckle family."

I know honeysuckle, I think, giving myself an imaginary pat on the back.

"Thrives in the damp, especially here by the river. And the bees like it."

I've been on the receiving end of his bee spiel many a time so to avoid another lecture, I remark, "It looks like a pincushion."

He tilts his head, not necessarily in agreement.

Yellow roses climb up the edge of the wall where the drainpipe runs. I reach up and rub a velvety petal between my fingertips. "Aren't roses hard to grow?"

"They can be temperamental but just like anything else, a wee bit of nurturing goes a long way."

A car passes, honking the horn.

"Who was that?"

"Wi you in that get up, hopefully naebody we know!"

Fearing being spotted in my exquisite garb, I pull off the hat and make for the side door.

"Right," dad says, brushing his hands together, crumbled earth falling to the ground. "Go and get ready so we can catch the next bus."

"How long does that give me?"

"Long enough."

The bus stop is located at the other end of Main Street, a scenic walk with occasional glimpses of the river through the tall pines that line one side of the road. Outside a row of bungalows, all with impeccable lawns, dad stops. I ask if he has a stone in his shoe.

"That's Ina," he says, nodding to an elderly woman, waving from inside the house. "Give her a wee wave."

I wave and Ina holds up her teacup in a gesture of cheers. I give her a thumbs up.

"She's a lovely wee soul," dad says, his focus still on Ina as he pats his hip and tips his head in question. Turning to me, he says, "She's no long after having her hip replaced."

Ina shrugs her narrow shoulders.

"Time," Dad mouths, tapping his watch. "Give it time." Ina nods in response and points from me to dad, gesturing, *Tall*.

"Takes after me," he mouths, moving his finger between us like a pendulum.

Ina points to the sky. Dad holds out his hand with his palm facing up.

"Still dry." He flips his hand over and trickles his fingers. "But rain later."

Ina gives one last wave. Dad and I do the same then continue walking.

A few doors down, he stops again.

"Who's that?" I ask as a well-dressed elderly man shuffles into window view.

"That's Bobby."

Very slowly, Bobby draws up his hunched body.

"He was a radioman in World War Two, ship was hit by a torpedo. Stories that'd make your hair curl. Walks with a cane but still tends to his garden."

"Wow," I gush, in awe of the fortitude of that generation.

"Great auld boy," dad says as Bobby blows a kiss.

I return the same and Bobby clutches at his heart. I laugh and blow another kiss. Bobby raises a gnarled finger to his lips, gesturing, *Don't tell your father!*

Dad raises his shoulders and curls his fists in a comical way. Bobby salutes then shuffles out of sight.

"Remind me to get him a pint of milk," dad says. "The rain will keep him in, the damp plays havoc wi his bad leg."

On we saunter, past the primary school, the inn, the bowling club and community hall. No sooner do we reach the bus stop when the sky blackens. I dart into the shelter and sit on the edge of the metal bench, cursing myself for wearing sandals more suited to a weekend on Nantucket than summer in Scotland. Rain begins to pelt against the Perspex shelter and dad makes a poor attempt at helping a woman gain control of a giant golf umbrella the wind seems intent on taking. I listen as she and dad chat good naturedly, seemingly oblivious to the fact they're getting drenched.

When the woman asks if I'm Tom and Liz's daughter, to my ear, it sounds like she's asking if I'm their doctor!

"Aye, that's oor Karen," dad replies with more than a hint of parental pride.

We begin chitchatting but all I can think about is the cold, gnawing its way in, through my pink polished toenails. I glance at my watch before pulling my sleeve down over my hand, commenting that the bus is late.

"That's guid," Muriel says, shaking drops of rain from her no longer coiffed hair.

I give her a questioning look.

"I'd have a heart attack if it was early!"

When the bus arrives, dad steps aside to allow Muriel on first. I follow her and the bus driver says, "Are you Tom's lassie fae America?" I nod in response.

"Well in that case," he chuckles, "The fare is triple!"

"Be nice to the braw lassie," Muriel chimes. "She's drookit and her taes are turning blue!"

The bus only has six rows, but with everyone talking ten to the dozen, up and down and across the aisle, it's lively. I listen to snippets of Isobel's present woes with the daughter-in-law she refers to as, the Loch

Ness moanster. There's general concern about, "The wee funny turn Malcolm took outside the phone box," and sighs of annoyance that, "The price of stamps is going up again."

When the bus pulls into the station, there's a hive of activity and a chorus of, "Cheerio, noo," as everyone goes their separate ways.

"The sun's threatening to come out," dad remarks, as we make our way back to the bus stop, laden with bags of groceries he insists upon carrying, my only contribution being the safekeeping of a box of strawberry tarts, leaving me a free hand to enjoy a sausage roll.

New faces line the bus stop, all of whom dad knows and all, it seems, with questions and comments about life in America.

"D'ye live near Disney? We were there last year wi the weans on their summer holidays. Loved it, especially the food," one woman says, patting her ample waistline.

"I'm much farther North," I explain. "About sixty miles outside of Boston, in an area called Cape Cod."

"Home of the Kennedy's," adds a newcomer. "Cursed family if ever there was one," he tuts.

Another woman tells me about her grandson who recently returned from New York. "Said he couldnae sleep for the din. Seems the taxis and sirens kept him up hauf the night but he said it was magic."

Kennedy man jibes me about the Boston Tea Party as if I were personally responsible. My eye roll is cut short when I catch dad glowering in my direction.

The mostly jovial chatter is interrupted when a sporty looking car screams to a halt. With half his body hanging out the window, a stringy youth screams, "Ya wee eejit, I nearly hit ye!"

Unfazed by her brush with an untimely death, the small dog continues across the road while the car speeds off, to a round of tittering, mostly pertaining to young people and the speed at which they drive.

The brown bundle plops down by my feet and looks up at me. I crouch down and rub her soft ears, then check her collar for a name or phone number, neither of which there are. I try to get dad's attention, but he and Kennedy curse man are fully engaged in a debate over, "The latest in health and safety fae they bampots in Brussels."

The dog leaps up expectantly when the bus comes into view and a young woman pushing a futuristic looking pram bumps against my precious cargo; the bag containing the box of strawberry tarts. She tugs back the rain cover to reveal a bundle of pink frills, out of which peer blue eyes.

"Angela," she states, thrusting the pink puff into my arms, with no explanation.

The doors on the bus fold open to a kerfuffle and Jimmy the driver says, "It's dee sert ed oan here, so dinnae bother folding the pram."

After dad and Kennedy man lift the pram onto the bus and slot it between the space allotted for luggage, dad gives me a hand up.

"Who's a good lassie?" he coos to Angela, before stepping off to retrieve the shopping bags.

Clutching Angela in all her candy floss glory, I gently toss the bag in the direction of the seat by the window when, suddenly, Angela arches her back then squirms, causing me almost to drop her. To steady the pair of us, I quickly plop onto the aisle seat, feeling the box and its gooey contents being crushed under my weight.

Grimacing, I propel my body forward and swiftly push the bag from under me. I slip off Angela's faux fur hood and spin her around to face the front of the bus. When she sees her mother, she starts wriggling and I hold her up, expecting to put her in her mother's arms but instead her mother holds out a bib.

"Stick that under her chin so she disnae slabber aw our yer nice coat."

Dad's last on the bus and while he's making his way up the aisle, I unravel the mangled bag and shove it on the floor. With a firm grasp of Angela's slippery coat, I scoot over to the window seat and use a tissue to wipe away a circle of condensation.

"See the doggie, Angela?"

Up ahead, Jimmy shouts, "C'mon Roxy," and the dog jumps on the bus and leaps up onto the front seat. I look at dad in question but all he says, is, "Jimmy makes her wait 'til everybody's on."

The door closes and the swell of chitter-chatter soon fills the air. When I unzip Angela's puffy coat, she lets out a little sigh and snuggles closer to me. I point out the animals in the fields and make exaggerated sounds she tries to mimic.

The bus slows and turns off the country road onto a dead-end street. Roxy lets out a loud bark that startles Angela, making her eyes widen and her mouth open to reveal two chiclet teeth. The bus moves at a snail's pace and I look at dad to see what's going on but he's engrossed in several conversations. I wipe the window again and watch in amazement as the bus squeezes down the street with barely an inch to spare.

An extremely small woman wearing an apron is sweeping the path of the four-in-a-block building and when the bus comes to a stop, she does the same. With broom in hand, she opens the gate, the timing of which coincides with the bus doors opening. Roxy jumps off the bus and sashays through the gate with her head held high.

"Ye should be inside wi yer feet up and the telly oan, ma!" Jimmy shouts.

The woman waves her hand dismissively. "Yer a long time deid."

"Hullo Harriet!" someone yells from behind, making me jump.

"Ma!" Jimmy hollers. "That's Cathy saying hullo."

"Oh, hullo Cathy, I cannae see ye wi the windaes aw steamed up." She gives a little wave then continues sweeping while Jimmy painstakingly reverses the bus down the street.

I look at dad. "What was that all about?"

Angela lets out a loud burp and starts fussing. "Your turn," I sing, passing her to dad.

"I'll take her, Tom," offers Kennedy curse man from across the aisle.

Before dad has a chance to delve into another discussion, I say, "The dog?"

"That's wee Roxy. She goes into town every day to get a few wee scraps from Jimmy's brother Gordon, the butcher, then Jimmy brings her home."

"Speaking of scraps," I grin, reaching down to retrieve the shopping bag. "How about some strawberry tart crumbs?"

MEGGIE & CHICO

I'm about to hang up the phone when mum's "Hullo?" booms across the Atlantic.

"Hi mum."

"Oh, it's yerself-"

A crashing sound cuts in, followed by dad shouting, "No, Chico! No!"

"This wee bizim's got me up to high doh!"

"Mum? What's going on? Are you there?"

"Och, it's bloody bedlam in here, the cat just knocked over that lovely vase you sent wi the flowers for ma birthday, the whole things in bloody smithereens. Tom!"

I wince at the thought of the shattered glass. "Wait, did you say *cat*?"

I hear the sound of the phone being dropped, followed by mum's voice in the background, her tone scolding. Dad picks up the phone. "Hiya, hen."

"Did you get a cat?"

"Aye, Chico. He's a lovely wee thing but he's into everything, you should see him climbing. He's like

Spiderman, only wi four legs. Mop this bit up by my feet Liz, I feel like I'm wading in the Clyde."

Meggie starts barking.

"He's driving Meggie mad wi his antics."

Meggie's symphonic barking turns to howling.

"Wait a wee minute, hen, I better take Meggie out, here's mum."

"Hullo?" Mum yells as though we're at opposite ends of the Chunnel.

"So, what's the deal-" I begin, but mum interrupts.

"Och, there he goes again, he loves jumping. I never knew cats were so agile. Poor wee Meggie, she just sits and watches him, probably wishes she could tumble her wilkies but that back leg is still giving her jip."

"When did you get the cat?" My tone is that of a kindergarten teacher, attempting to get the attention of the class. On the first day.

After Tini went to the rainbow bridge at the age of seventeen, my parents swore they'd never get another dog. Then, while mum was visiting family in Glasgow, she walked to the local shop, where, "A manky wee dug wi eyes the size of saucers wearing a velvet collar dotted wi plastic rhinestones," sat tied to the lamp post. According to the shop keeper, the dog was already there when he opened up at the crack of dawn and that it wasn't uncommon for dogs to be left abandoned in that very spot. Mum bought a can of Chum that she fed to the dog by hand, then she untied the rope and, "Took her up the park for a wee donner." Suspecting that the dog was indeed abandoned, mum promised the shopkeeper she'd return at the end of the day and when she did, "The poor wee soul was still there wi her tail tucked between her legs."

Whenever mum returned from Glasgow, dad would meet her at the bus stop. He relayed the story of mum coming off the bus, "Wi a wee scrawny looking thing wi big brown eyes." Dad had only to hear the words, "Left tied to a lamppost," before promptly falling in love.

Mum planned on calling her Maggie but when she told Will about her on the phone, his American accent pronounced the name as Meggie.

To say my parents doted on Meggie would go beyond understatement. The first time I met her, I joked that it was my first experience with sibling rivalry but one look was all it took for her to secure her place as the four-legged sister I never had.

"We had no intention of getting another pet," mum continues, "but a few of the local lads showed up wi him the other day."

"What lads?"

"D'ye remember that wee group who sit on the bridge by the shops?"

It takes a second for me to register who she's referring to. During my first visit to the village, dad asked if I, "Fancied going for a wee walk." Keen to see the local landscape, I slipped my feet into the two sizes too big wellies mum left by the side door ("I found them in the charity shop and they still had the label on them, some designer name. I don't know how they can justify asking that much for two bits of rubber.")

That *wee walk* turned into a trek to the next village, where dad pointed out a group of young men, gathered on the bridge. Every morning they'd show up in the hope of being picked up for a day or more of work with one of the local tradesmen. Dad stopped to chat with the lads, all of whom seemed down in the dumps, unemployment being as it is in many parts of Scotland.

"So, on Tuesday morning," mum continues, "The lads were on the bridge waiting for Alistair. You know Alistair, the painter, apparently he won the pools a few years back and spent it aw on booze which I'm sure is true coz he always looks oot his face. In the pub the night before, he said he needed four lads for a big job at some la di da place in the West End, but when Alistair showed up, *late and hungover*, he said he only needed one of them."

I have no idea who Alistair is. Nor if he won the lottery. Or has a drinking problem.

"The lads are keen to work and make a few bob but it's no easy. Anyway, a big flash car drove by and stopped at the end of the road. Next thing, the door opened and somebody pushed the cat oot."

"Ugh," I groan. "That's so cruel."

"Aye, well needless to say whoever it was drove away. The lads made their way towards the cat and Kenny, d'ye remember him, handsome big guy, hair like, who's the actor that was in Braveheart?"

"Mel Gibson?"

"Aye, him. Anyway, Kenny popped into the shop and bought a tin of cat food. It's daylight robbery in that wee place but in this instance it couldnae be helped. Next thing Morag fae the bakers, d'ye remember her, moody Morag they call her. Nice enough lassie but I think she's a wee bit do lally. Anwyay, she came oot wi a big bowl of milk, smiling apparently, which is shocking because she's usually got a face like fizz."

Visions of William Wallace and Moody Morag cloud my brain as mum continues.

"The lads sat wi the cat for a wee while hoping whoever abandoned him might have a change of heart."

"Seems pretty obvious that wasn't about to happen," I chime.

"Aye, I know. I'll never understand people like that but it happens all the time. Look at wee Meggie."

"Now living in the lap of luxury. So, how did *you* end up with the cat?"

"Crabbit Colin, that's whit they call him, suggested they ask around to see if anybody recognized him so they started walking and before they knew it, they were here."

"That's a long walk."

"Nah, it's only about four miles. Anyway, dad and I were sitting doon by the river, enjoying a wee piece on that lovely bread you always buy when yer here, whit's it called again?"

"Ciabatta?"

"Aye that's it. Dad said he'll get more next time he goes shopping."

"Mum! The cat!"

"Oh aye, so we were outside and ye know how everybody stops here once they come over the bridge. Kenny was carrying the cat and I asked whit its name

41

was. He shouted, 'It's a cheeky wee thing,' but I thought he said Chico, so when they got to the gate, I said, 'Hello Chico'".

Mum is notorious for believing she heard one thing, only to discover it was something else entirely.

"Kenny put him in my arms and the wee soul cooried right into me."

"But you've always had a fear of cats."

"D'ye remember that time in Milton Keynes when a cat got in through the wee windae in the downstairs lav?"

"How could I forget? You almost screamed the place down!"

"Aye well you know that's where I used to pray a lot, whit was it you called it?"

"Your confession box."

She chuckles. "Oof, if they walls could talk!"

"So...Chico?"

"He looked up at me and I knew right there and then we had to help him. Dad was taken wi him as well, oh you should see him, he's a wee cracker, pure white fluff wi one black stripe."

"Aw, he sounds gorgeous."

"He was purring away and dad asked the lads whit they were planning to do wi him. They'd asked all over the place if anybody recognized him but it was obvious he'd been abandoned."

"Awful," I utter.

"Tuesday was a scorcher, we tried sitting oot the day before, the sun was shining but the wind would've cut ye in two."

I shudder at the visual!

"The other guy, oh I cannae remember his name, nice guy as well, a wee bit on the hefty side but I think that's fae the bevvy. He asked if we were interested in keeping the cat. Dad and I looked at each other and I said, 'Aye we'll take him, but if ye hear who's cat he is we'll give him back.'"

"Obviously."

"Dad gave them each a cold lager and och you would've thought *they'd* won the pools. They were all smiles, it was hot mind you."

"So, that was what, three days ago?"

"Aye and we've no heard a peep so I think he's oors to keep. I was talking to Olive in the shop, d'ye remember her? Olive the nurse? Long black hair? Always asks for ye."

"No, I don't think I-"

"Aye, ye do. Anyway, she said the best thing to do wi a new cat, is cover its paws in butter."

"Butter?"

"Aye, apparently if you cover their paws in butter it makes them stay in the hoose."

I'm so confused, I don't respond. Meggie starts barking again.

"Och, is that you back?" Mum says, presumably to dad.

"Hello again."

"Hello dad, mum just told me the story of how you got the cat but what's all this about the butter?"

Dad lets out a hearty laugh. "Oh wait 'til ye hear this yin. Olive, you know Olive, the nurse, always asks for ye. Lovely looking lassie, looks a bit like Crystal Gayle."

Crystal Gayle!

"She told mum to put butter on Chico's paws because wherever a cat cleans itself is where it feels at home, so it won't wander off."

"I haven't heard that before," I say, the lyrics to "Don't it make my brown eyes blue," floating through my head.

"Apparently it works. However, mum, being mum, got a wee bit carried away and *slathered* Chico's paws in sooo much butter he was slipping and sliding all over the place!"

I'm laughing so hard I can't speak. Visions of mum, Lurpak in hand, chasing the cat around the kitchen.

"She's sum wumin sure she is? Still, the cat seems happy as Larry here, so hopefully he can stay. I better get Meggie, here's mum again."

"Mum, how much butter did you use on Chico's paws?" I hear her chewing.

"What are you eating?"

She swallows loudly. "Something..." She swallows again. "You love."

I laugh. "I love lots of things."

"Strawberry tarts. I just found them in the fridge when I was getting Chico his milk. Dad must've bought them this morning, they're delishio!"

A pang of homesickness washes over me and, more than anything, I wish I could climb through the phone, from my kitchen to theirs. I'd sit at the kitchen table, eating strawberry tarts (yes, plural) with lashings of tea, laughing at the antics of Meggie and Chico as they run rings around my parents.

"Mum, I'll let you get going. I'll phone you in a few days, ok?"

"Aye ok Karen, tell everybody we send our love."

"Will do. Bye mum. Take care. Love you."

Just before I hang up there's an almighty clatter, followed by mum, hollering, "Tom! Catch him!"

WEDDING BELLES

I'm sitting at the bottom of the garden, wrapped in a blanket, my hands circling a mug of tea, in the hopes it'll heat me up. Dad's wading through the river, his eyes scanning for rocks to add to the patio he's building. Clad in shorts and a sweatshirt with the sleeves cut off, he looks like an extra from Dirty Dancing, sparking my '80's brain to recall the line, "Nobody puts baby in the corner."

"The water's been shallow all week," he says, cutting into my senseless train of thought as he picks up a boulder for inspection. "Unlike last week when the storms were a brewing and a washing machine." He stops and stares at me. "I kid you not, a *bloody washing machine* went flying past. I thought I was seeing things!"

In the area of the garden mum refers to as, "The wee sun trap," she's asleep, her body splayed across the sun lounger, her diamante encrusted sunglasses perched on top of her head. From time to time a weak (and I stress, *weak!*) ray of sun catches one of the sparkles, creating a laser effect that extends in my direction.

Willing it to miraculously shoot some warmth through me, I open my palm to the beam.

"Are ye still cold?" Dad asks.

"This is warming me up," I lie, raising the mug.

"Ye might be coming down wi something."

Nothing serious! Just hypothermia!

"Did ye put honey in yer tea?"

I shake my head no.

"There's a wee jar in the kitchen, on the window sill. Cliff the beekeeper drops a jar off every now and again. Mum's no too keen on him, she thinks he's a numpty but I think he's just the loner type."

If only to humour dad, I get up and, with the blanket trailing behind like a wooly train, I make my way up the garden path. In the kitchen, I find the jar of honey exactly where dad said it would be (the man is nothing if not fastidious.) I unscrew the sticky lid (mum's doing) and take a good whiff of the rich, amber goo. I find cutlery in the third drawer I open and plunge a teaspoon deep into the jar.

Waiting for the honey to dissolve, I tap the window. Dad looks up and I raise the jar, gesturing, *Do you want some in your tea?* He gives a thumbs up before returning to the task at hand. When the tea kettle clicks off, I hear the sound of hooves, clip clopping. I look out the window to the other side of the bridge, where, through the thicket of birch trees, I glimpse two white horses pulling a carriage.

Abandoning the tea, I dash outside. Dad's at the water's edge, balancing on one foot, shaking the other dry, before slipping into a pair of sandals I would never have imagined him wearing.

"Quick!" He shouts. "Wake mum up!"

Before I can finish saying, "Wedding," mum's eyes shoot open. Bolting upright, she exclaims, "I was dreaming aboot horses!"

"Wasn't a dream," I say, pointing in the direction of the horses as they close in. We watch as two coachmen, both in top hats, guide the horses over the narrow bridge.

"Take that blanket off!" Mum hisses.

"Why?" I sulk. "It's not like I'm going to the wedding."

The carriage is open top and the bride gives a little ceremonial wave. Mum smiles her widest smile and waves but the second the horses are out of sight, she turns her attention to dad. "Tom! Ye should've woke me up earlier and I thought I told ye to throw they sandals away! Sometimes I swear I'd be better talking to the bridge." Her eyes dart from the church to the washing line, strewn with towels and a few items of clothing. "Right!" she orders, gesturing for me to open my arms. "This all has to go before the guests arrive!"

Forcefully she begins unclipping the wooden pegs and I open my arms to receive the laundry, most of which is still damp. "See these tartan socks," she growls. "I told dad to bin them ages ago!"

From inside the cottage, Meggie barks when a coach that takes up most of the road pulls up outside the church.

"Dump this lot in the bath!" Mum barks. "Now skeedaddle!"

Feeling excited at the prospect of the wedding about to unfold, I take my place on the couch, the back of which rests up against the sash window. Mum scurries past as the piper, clad in a Black Watch tartan kilt, begins serenading the bevy of well-heeled guests as they enter the church.

A few minutes later, mum comes into the living room wearing a yellow sundress patterned with large daisies. Slowly, she twists a circular hairbrush through her hair, all the while bending to the side as though she's two feet taller than her regular five two. She quickly gives up on the hair and pulls earrings from her dress pocket.

"Are those the earrings I gave you for Christmas?" I ask, my eyes flitting from mum to the church, not wishing to miss a moment of the wedding action. She nods and tells me to, "Budge over." She rolls the brush through her hair once more, then she untangles it and stuffs it under the cushion.

"*Your* hair could do wi a wee brush," she scoffs, retrieving the hairbrush.

Dad's attempt at passing through the living room to the bedroom fails when mum asks if he'll, "Make us a wee cup of tea."

"Yes, your majesty," he says with a mock bow. "But first I must discard my common clothing!" He flashes me a look that says, *Just wait! It'll only get worse!*

The piper strikes up again, the same tune as before and I look at mum in question. She shakes her head dismissively. "That's Simon, poor wee soul, he only knows a few tunes. His da is usually the one to play, but he's probably at another wedding. June brides and all that."

I crane my neck to see farther up the road. "I wonder where the bride went?"

Mum rolls her eyes. "She was far too early. Poor planning."

Dad comes into the living room. "Who's that sharp dressed man?" I chirp, noting the sheen on his freshly polished shoes.

Dad glances out the window. "Bride was too early. She's obviously as keen as you were to marry me, Lizzie."

"Aye, right," mum smirks, swiping the thigh of his pressed blue trousers when he bends to gives her a peck on the cheek. I get up and check my hair in the gilt framed mirror above the fireplace. It looks a little windswept so I smooth it down. In my peripheral vision, I sense mum giving me the up down. "Should I change my clothes?"

"Nah, yer fine. I like that top, royal blue suits ye, much better than all that black ye wear."

The time passes and the young piper shuffles nervously from foot to foot. The minister pops his head out the church door and the piper points in the direction of the hill. It's another ten minutes before the Rolls Royce pulls up, catching the piper off guard. He fumbles with one of the chanters, then gives up and stands at attention as three women, all resembling the bride, walk slowly up the path, laughing in unison when the breeze catches the trumpet hem on their periwinkle dresses.

The sound of the horses draws me closer to the window.

"That's more like it," mum remarks, shimmying her shoulders.

One of the coachmen gives the bride's father a hand navigating the steps and he, in turn, holds out his hand to his daughter. When the bride stands up, mum tuts disapprovingly.

"What?" I ask.

"I don't like her dress."

"Really? I think it's stunning. So elegant and look how pretty she is."

Mum shakes her head. "Too thin."

Dad comes into the living room carrying a tray laden with tea and biscuits. "Will there be anything else ma'am? Ma'am as in ham not spam!" he jokes, setting down the tray on the coffee table.

With the tea gone and only a few biscuits remaining, dad looks at his watch. "Shouldnae be more than a few more minutes, unless Ian-"

"Who's Ian?" I ask.

"The minister. Nice enough guy-"

"But he's a bit of a gab," mum cuts in.

"Looks like the piper's getting ready to strike up again." No sooner are my words out when the teen puts the blowpipe to his mouth. It takes a few seconds before I recognize the tune.

"Oh, I love this one!" I exclaim, jumping up off the couch.

"Mairi's Wedding," mum beams, as I pull her up.

In a poor imitation of the Highland Fling, we dance around the living room, singing:

> *Step we gaily on we go, heel for heel and toe for toe, arm in arm and on we go, all for Mairi's wedding.*
> *Over hillways up and down myrtle green and bracken brown, pass the shillings through the town, all for the sake of Mairi.*

"You two," dad laughs, gathering up the tray.

Mum and I plop back on the couch, catching our breath as the guests continue spilling out of the church.

"Nothing better than a wee jig," she chuckles, fanning her flushed face.

"Where's the bride and groom? Don't they usually come out first?"

Mum shakes her head. "They'll wait 'til everybody's outside."

At the sight of the happy couple, cheers go up and confetti begins to fly.

"Aw, I love confetti," I sigh. "Will they have a scramble?"

"I'm no sure," mum says. "I think that might just be a Glesga thing. You used to love that when you were a wee lassie."

"Are you saying I'm too big for a scramble?"

She laughs. "That'd be something, you elbowing the wee yins oot the way."

"Maybe I could use the money to buy a hairbrush," I tease.

"Showtime, Lizzie," dad announces, brushing imaginary crumbs off his shirt. I look out to see the photographer leading the newlyweds and wedding party in the direction of the cottage. Mum pulls a tube of lipstick from her dress pocket and liberally applies the pale pink to her lips. Smacking her lips together, she fluffs up her blonde bob.

"Are you two planning on being in the wedding pictures? Or are you renewing your vows and forget to tell me?"

They ignore me and make their way outside, just as the photographer reaches the gate.

"Thomas! Elizabeth!" he coos in a plummy English accent. "How delightful to see you both again. May I introduce the happy couple, Hamish and Henrietta, very dear friends of mine."

I watch in amusement as pleasantries are exchanged, covering my mouth so they won't hear me giggling when mum says, "Your dress is stunning."

One by one, the wedding party step through the gate, each person stopping to shake hands with my parents, thanking them profusely for their, "Terribly generous use of the garden."

I move to the side window for a better look, crouching a little to avoid being seen. Up close, the bride is dainty. The bodice of her dress is swathed in sculpted lace, with embroidered miniature rosebud buttons lining the back. *Definitely not off the rack.* The groom has clearly been preparing for his wedding day by gorging on everything and although he's probably about thirty, most of his ginger hair is already gone.

I watch as Anthony the photographer (mum has uttered his name at least a dozen times) choreographs what will no doubt be an exquisite wedding album, with the trailing ivy on the sandstone bridge and shimmering water providing the perfect backdrop. The entire scene is so appealing it makes me wish I'd insisted upon getting married in Scotland instead of snow blanketed New Hampshire.

Looking like the cat who got the cream, dad saunters into the living room swinging a bottle of Glenmorangie.

"You, sir," I drawl, "were obviously aware of today's events."

"That's right," he nods, placing the bottle on the mantle. "Anthony approached us a few weeks ago and needless to say mum was smitten." He shakes his head and chortles.

After her long, drawn out goodbye with Anthony, mum comes barging into the living room. "They were lovely, weren't they?"

"A wee bit pan loafy," dad teases. "But nice."

"You can both get back into your peasant togs now!" I laugh.

"Not so fast," dad smirks. "There's another wedding at two."

CHURCH KEY

It's April school vacation and dad and Will are out walking Meggie, a pastime my son embraces only in Scotland. Mum's visiting a poorly neighbour and I'm engrossed in the latest in the Outlander series by Diana Gabaldon, all the while hoping Jamie Fraser will accidentally fall through a standing stone and appear at the front door.

Filling the time before Jamie shows up and turns my world upside down, I feel compelled to write something of a romantic nature, using the cottage as the central character. The blank pages of my journal taunt me to fill them with words of passion drawn from what mum calls, "Karen's big busy brain."

The honk from a passing car distracts me so I put down the pen and drain the last of the tea dregs. Using my fingertip, I wipe the remaining crumbs from the now barren plate of biscuits, something I won't be doing after Jamie shows up! With story ideas far exceeding a PG13 rating, I sigh a deep sigh and allow my head to loll back on the couch. The soothing trickle of the river filters through the billowing net curtain and I close my eyes.

The sound of a dog barking rouses me from a particularly satisfying dream, causing me, in my state of annoyance, to look out the window. In the churchyard, dad is talking animatedly to a middle-aged couple, dressed for an expedition to the Arctic. Next to Will, Meggie sits obediently, willing him to drop a chip in her direction. The nearest chippy is a few miles away, which explains their lengthy absence.

Dad is pointing to the ancient jougs, no doubt bamboozling the couple with historical facts about the iron collars used to punish and shame the locals for any civil or ecclesiastical crimes. As many times as I've heard the stories of the jougs, a shiver still runs through me at the thought of being padlocked into such for an extended period of time.

With all hope of Jamie's presence completely dashed, I get up and see dad and Will crossing the street. Dad tousles Will's hair and says something that makes him laugh. When they reach the gate, dad whistles like he always does, letting mum know he's home.

Meggie bursts into the living room and makes a beeline for me. I flop onto the couch, taking her head in my lap.

"Who's a good pup e?" I use the high-pitched voice I reserve for every dog I've ever known. Meggie's wildly wagging tail swats the corner of the table, narrowly missing the mug.

"It's empty," I say in response to dad's glance.

"I was just talking to a couple from Australia."

"Are they here on holiday?"

Dad nods as he retrieves a huge iron key from the back of the mantle.

"Whoa, what's that for?"

"The church," he says nonchalantly. "Come and meet them if you want."

I follow him into the kitchen, automatically switching on the tea kettle before stepping out the side door. Will looks up from the water's edge.

"Hey, mom."

"Hi buddy, how are you?"

"Good," he nods, stuffing the empty newspaper wrapper into his fleece jacket pocket.

"Chips all gone?"

"Yeah," he drawls. "Meggie ate them all."

"Ah, dogs and their thumbs," I joke, making him smile. "I'm just popping over to the church with granda, you ok here?"

"Sure," he says, returning his attention to the rock he skips, once, twice, three times, before it lands with a splash, halfway across the water.

"You ready, dad?" I ask, slipping my feet into the wellies mum keeps, rain or shine, outside the kitchen door.

Intently thumbing his way through a stack of papers on the kitchen table, dad looks, as mum would say, "All business," so I leave him to it and go down to the river, where Will and I shout encouragingly to Meggie, as she thunders through the water.

"That's us," dad says, waving some papers. "This is a list of the gravestones." He continues talking as we make our way across the street. "The Aussie guys great-grandparents were married in the church, also buried there in eighteen eighty-two and four."

"Incredible," I utter.

"I told them you and mum have been to Australia but I couldnae remember if you went to Melbourne."

Clive and Estelle are both mild mannered and he, especially, seems a little overwhelmed to be in the place that marks such a significant part of his family history. They talk about how life got in the way of them coming to the spot they've longed to visit for many years, an all too common story, regardless of where you come from.

Dad leads us up the path to the old section of the cemetery, where many of the stone bases have crumbled, causing the headstones to tilt. I cross my fingers, hoping their family stone is still standing proud. Dad points to an upright slab a few feet away, the moss infested base the only indication of age, the names and dates still legible.

"That's it there," he says, quietly.

Clive and Estelle join hands and I take a step forward. Dad puts out his arm to stop me. He shakes his head and without speaking, says, *leave them to it.*

I follow dad to the side door of the church and watch as he finagles the key in the lock. From the gravesite I hear Estelle's muffled sobs. The church door creaks open and dad steps to the side. With a stone floor and no heat source, the chilled air makes me shiver. With my arms crossed, I wander around, stopping in front of the pulpit, flanked on either side by two tall stained-glass windows, each bearing the coat of arms of two local families.

"Who doesn't appreciate stained glass," I remark. "Especially the warmth it emanates."

Dad chuckles. "You'll never be able to live in Scotland ever again."

"I dinnae ken wit ye mean." My attempt at an Ayrshire accent fails miserably, making dad laugh even more. We gaze at the windows and he opens his mouth to speak but changes his mind. Being my mother's daughter, I ask what he wanted to say.

"I was just thinking about how far that couple have come."

I know what it's like to fly through the night, sitting squashed in a seat next to a sleeping stranger you daren't disturb for a toilet visit. Willing the hours to pass quickly so you can return to the people you love and the landscapes that still show up in your dreams.

With our gaze still on the stained glass, dad recites a passage from his favourite Robert Burns poem, "Ae Fond Kiss."

> *Had we never loved so kindly. Had we never loved so blindly. Never met, or never parted. We'd never have been broken hearted.*

Clive and Estelle appear in the doorway.

"Come on in," dad says cheerfully.

They're both wiping at their eyes. Clive shakes dad's hand heartily and pats him on the back.

"We can't thank you enough..." his voice trembles.

"We'll never forget this," Estelle says, joining us at the pulpit.

Never one for praise, dad awkwardly accepts their gestures of gratitude.

The four of us stand in silence, each lost in our own memories. Dad's parents are long gone, as are the majority of his fourteen siblings. Seeing all of this cross his face, I'm gripped by a strong sense of the meaning of family.

Mum's burst of, "Coo-e!" echoes around the church and snaps me back to the present.

"A wee birdie told me ye were here," she says, wiping her feet on the mat before stepping inside.

"My wife, Liz," dad grins.

"And Will," mum beams as Will steps out from behind her. "Oh and the kettle's on! Ye must be gasping for a wee cuppa tea. Will told me you've come all the way from Australia? Did Tom tell ye Karen and I went there when she worked for British Airways? Och, that Sydney Opera House is something isn't it, whit a place! We loved the beaches in Perth but ma favourite thing was cuddling the wee koala bears." She clutches at her heart. "Och, I just loved them!"

Mum's still holding court when I slip out the door to the cemetery, a place filled with stories of love and loss, etched in names and dates of birth and death, separated by the all-important dash, the place where it all happens. The place where we live our lives, all the while knowing we are connected to the past and that no matter how far we travel, we're always drawn back, to home.

HEAVY HEART

Roughly seven hours after departing from the east coast of America, the plane begins its descent towards Glasgow airport. There's a deep orange glow in the dawn winter sky and I know that somewhere down there is where my story began. It's where I was born, where my parents were born, their parents and also theirs. It's the place where my parents met, fell in love and got married.

Somewhere down there, in a town bordered by parcels of green pasture, lies my father's dead body. I wonder if anyone is at the funeral home, or if he's alone. It feels wrong that he might be there alone.

In an attempt to prolong the inevitable, I wait until the last minute to disembark, thankful that the crew have given up on bidding the passengers farewell. My lead legs lead me up the long corridor, through immigration, where a cheery faced woman my age checks my passport and says, "Welcome home."

Standing by the baggage carousel, I think about the countless times I've lingered there, with my now fifteen-year old son. I smile at the memory of his cherubic face lighting up whenever his tiny suitcase would appear. Remembering the anticipation I felt knowing my parents would be waiting for us beyond the doors springs tears to my eyes.

Not now, I think. Definitely not now.

The double glass doors open and Patrick comes towards me. Patrick is my cousin who lives in Glasgow, a few streets away from where he grew up. The last time I saw him was a few years ago, at his wedding.

"I'm awful sorry about your da," he offers, enveloping me in a hearty hug. "He was one in a million."

I follow Patrick outside to a drizzly day with sky the colour of steel. Sorrow catches my throat. "Hang on a sec," I say, fiddling with the zipper on my boot, buying time to choke back the tears. I don't want to leave the safety of the airport. I want to stay here, where the plane can take me home and I can pretend none of this is happening.

When we reach Patrick's car, I automatically go to the driver's side.

"Yer no in America noo," he teases. I shake my head, appreciating his attempt at lightening the mood. I go to the passenger side and Patrick tosses my sparsely filled suitcase on the back seat.

"Thanks for picking me up."

"Ach, it's nae bother. I've no been oot that way fur ages but I've got this new sat nav." He fumbles with the small device. "I bought it aff a wee guy in the pub last night so I've no had time to…"

His voice trails off as a series of beeps bring the device to life. The screen lights up and Patrick grunts a sound of satisfaction, then the screen turns black. He growls in frustration as he makes another attempt to get it to work.

"That tea should still be hot but I don't know whit's in the poke. I told the lassie at the bakers ma cousin was arriving fae America and she'd probably be gasping fur some fine Scottish fare." I catch his smile. "There should be a few wee sachets of sugar if ye need them."

I remove the lid and greedily gulp down half the contents. The milky brew coats my throat, making me sigh in satisfaction.

"Ah, I really needed that. Thanks."

"There's no much a good cup of Scottish tea, or for that matter, a few wee haufs cannae fix, is there?"

I smile in response to Patrick's heartfelt expression as he continues in his quest to make sense of the sat nav.

"Uff, I'm no getting anywhere wi this bloody thing."

To let Patrick know I'm still his cousin from Glasgow I ask, "Did it not come with instructions?"

Patrick laughs a hearty laugh, because we both know that when you, "Buy something aff a wee guy in the pub," it doesn't come in the box.

"I'm sure I can get us there from memory," I offer, knowing full well I could walk there with my eyes shut.

"We might be better aff just doing that. Besides, if we get lost, we've guid Scottish tongues in oor heids."

It's early Saturday morning and driving through the quiet city roads, Patrick regales me with amusing stories about his toddler son. His easy manner and sense of humour remind me why we were so close growing up and makes me feel nostalgic for carefree childhood days.

It doesn't take long before we're out on the open road, where every turn presents another spectacular vista of snow peaked munros that bring to mind drizzled icing on a cake fresh out of the oven.

When the sign for the village comes into view my stomach somersaults knowing I'm less than a hundred feet from my mother. I crack open the window to the sound of the streams my son and I have meandered alongside, my father urging us to dip our toes in, our squeals loud enough to wake the dead.

Patrick slows considerably as he rounds the bend, to where the little stone cottage, built in 1740, proudly sits next to the bridge. With a newly installed slate roof guaranteed for 250 years, the cottage represents longevity, but knowing it's where my father took his last breath a few nights before, I blurt, "Can you keep driving?"

Patrick glances in my direction and opens his mouth to speak but instead he nods and continues down Main Street.

We pass the homes of people I've come to know well during my many visits. We drive past the red sandstone school, the inn, the bowling club, the community hall and the shop. I sense Patrick waiting for me to ask him to turn around but I'm not ready for the reality of what's to come.

A few miles later, he pulls over. With both hands on the steering wheel, he blows out a stream of air. "I'm sorry, I don't know whit to do. Just tell me whit ye need."

"Just give me a minute," I say, opening the door.

Patrick cuts the engine and the silence is soothing. The slate grey sky meets the expanse of green, dotted with tiny blobs of sheep. Inhaling deeply, I smell the promise of heavy rain, looking upward, for what I'm not sure.

Patrick joins me and wraps my coat around my shoulders. We stand in silence, our breath mingling in the frigid air. When my teeth begin to chatter, he ushers me back to the car.

Mum is standing outside the front door. She's wearing a bright pink bathrobe with silver moons, clutching each of her shoulders with the opposite hand. Patrick's sister steps out of the cottage, her expression solemn.

I don't want to go inside. He isn't here anymore. It'll never be the same again. I can't go in. I want to go home.

I step through the gate and open my arms to my mother. Softly, she squeezes my arm, turns, and goes inside.

Meggie sniffs me wildly and when I bend to pat her, she jumps up and licks my clammy face. I slip off my coat and a sharp pain shoots through my stomach when I toss it over the phone chair, where my father used to sit.

I open the window to the January chill as my cousins bend their heads together and speak in hushed tones. I sit on the couch next to mum and take her cold hand in mine. Gently, I rub my thumb over the brown spots on her hand and we stare at the embers in the fireplace.

"You have to pick a suit out for dad," she says, breaking the silence. She pushes herself up off the couch and gestures for me to follow her. In the bedroom, she points to the wardrobes that line the back wall. "On the right," she says, shuffling out of the bedroom.

I go to the side of the bed where my father slept throughout their forty-five years of marriage. I pick up his pillow and hold it close to me. Wave after wave of memories crowd my thoughts and I feel myself sway. My overloaded mind swirls with questions only my mother can answer:

Were you with him?
Was he in pain?
Did he know what was happening?
How long did it take?
Did you tell him you love him?

The pillow slips out of my arms onto the floor and I ease open the wardrobe doors. Each item of clothing faces the same way mine do, three thousand miles away.

"We are the same," I whisper, thumbing my way through pressed shirts and tailored jackets. My hand rests on a dark wool suit that feels soft from wear. The black tie wrapped around the hanger suggests recent attendance at a funeral, probably one of the elderly locals.

It's important to pay your respects.

Knowing this is the suit, I remove it and hold it up to the window, a ray of light confirming it's the right choice. I shut my eyes and imagine my father crossing the road, hearing him whistle when he opens the gate.

I pick out a shirt and take it, with the suit, into the living room. My cousins react as if seeing my newborn baby for the first time. Their enthusiasm is wrong for the occasion, but I understand why they do it. Patrick's sister asks if I've included underwear and socks and I look at her, dumbfounded. The request seems absurd but this world is new to me so I go back into the bedroom.

In the top drawer, I find a pack of handkerchiefs my son sent my father for Christmas. I tear open the pack and add one of the white cotton handkerchiefs to the small pile. My father never left the house without, "A fresh hankie," and I don't want him going away without one.

No sooner do my cousins depart, when mum retreats to the place she always goes when the demons are upon her. I tuck her in and close the blind.

The paint on the outside windowsills is peeling and the loose cobblestones on the path leave me wishing I'd been there to witness the signs of my father's deteriorating health. The river runs high with a mesmerizing force I don't ever remember and I focus my attention on it, hoping to block out the sound of the phone, ringing nonstop, in the kitchen

One of the neighbours, a retired psychiatrist and good friend of mum's, stops by. It's obvious from the questions she asks that mum has shared her history of her time in, "The dark tunnel." Muriel scribbles her phone number on the back of a bus timetable and makes me promise that I'll call her, day or night.

Meggie's on the bed, with her body curled around mum's feet. I switch on the bedside lamp, taking care not to knock over the ceramic angel that's graced mum's bedside table for as long as I can remember. I stroke mum's shoulder but her soft snore tells me she's asleep. I remove the cup of stone-cold tea, throw away the toast and replenish the glass of water.

After I unplug the phone, I curl up on the phone chair with Chico. He stares into my face as though deciphering my every emotion. Wrought with sadness over this cruel new reality, my thoughts turn to the events of the past few days, starting with the late-night phone call when mum screamed the words that changed everything.

My eyes scan the framed pictures that dominate every surface. Pictures of a young Will and my father, skipping rocks, matching grins of satisfaction. Pictures of Cape Cod beaches, summer smiles against vivid blue skies, Will sandwiched between my parents, ice-cream dripping from his fingers. Pictures of me in my starched school uniform, my hair long and silky, with a lopsided smile that screamed, "shy." A black and white picture of my paternal grandparents, standing stiffly outside their home, strangers to the camera. My father hanging out the window, a cheeky smirk plastered across his seven-year old face, ready to take on the world.

Long after the pets have called it a day, I crawl into bed beside my mother. The smell of brandy shrouds her and a wave of anger pulses through me but, given the circumstances, I don't act upon it, instead making a mental note to find the bottle.

I take mum's hand in mine and she opens her eyes. I put the glassy look in her eyes down to exhaustion and take a deep breath to calm myself before I say something I might regret. Despair threads through my every cell and there's so much I want to ask and so much I want to say, but the words, "We need to pray," are the ones that tumble out.

Mum gives a slight nod of acknowledgement and for the first time in a long time, I begin to recite, "The Lord's Prayer." It's hard to speak through the tears but whenever I falter, mum squeezes my hand and I keep going. I pray for strength for what's to come, for mum's safety and for God to guide my father safely home.

LILIES

Mum coos words of praise to Meggie and Chico as they circle her feet under the kitchen table. "Whit'll happen to these two wee rascals?"

I'm at the sink filling the tea kettle. "I don't know, but don't worry, I'll make sure they each go to a good home." I turn around to let her see my forced *everything's going to be ok* expression, quickly turning back after I see the sadness that clings to her sunken cheeks.

"When are ye going home? Ye need to get home to Will."

I mumble something about not knowing, knowing full well I can't leave until mum is in a safe place.

With the exception of perfunctory toilet visits, this is the second time mum has been out of bed since my father's funeral, almost two weeks ago. Before the kettle has a chance to boil, I hear the chair scraping across the floor. My heart sinks, knowing she's going back to bed.

I have countless memories of sitting with mum while she's in bed, either at home or in hospital, her eyes swollen from crying over things she had little or no control over. Sometimes, I'd do my homework, trying to engage her while she stared at the ceiling. In other settings, I'd murmur soothing words, averting my eyes from the bandage wrapped tightly around her wrist.

Mum bypasses the bed and flings open the wardrobe doors, the action of which causes my father's clothes to sway to an imaginary upbeat tempo. Tugging clothes from hangers, mum tosses everything onto the bed, her accompanying commentary raspy and rapid.

"I don't know whit possessed him to buy this coat, he never wore it."

"D'ye remember this shirt? We bought it at Filene's Basement in Boston."

"Nana gave him this tie years ago, paisley pattern was all the rage at the time."

"This jacket will never go out of fashion. D'ye think Will would have any use for it?"

"I always loved him in green. Matched his eyes."

With her frenetic pace, it doesn't take long before the bed is piled high and when it seems there's no more space, she says, "The bin bags are under the sink." I take this as my cue to retrieve them and when I return, she tells me to, "Shove everything in the bags."

The way she says it doesn't require an answer but I don't want to do this. I'm not ready to start erasing anything related to my father.

Once the wardrobe is bereft of any and all traces of her husband, mum wedges herself between two piles. I'm half expecting her to fall back in exhaustion but instead she reaches over to the dresser drawer. Working with the same frenzied abandon, she tosses each article of clothing over her shoulder. I stack the things I want to keep but everything else goes into the bags.

When the drawers are empty, mum eyes the shoe stand and hands me a bag. One pair at a time, she drops my father's shoes into the bag. The sound of each shoe hitting the floor makes me flinch.

"Go and get me the Ajax that's under the kitchen sink," she barks. "And a few dish rags. This place is a bloody mess!"

With my heart pounding, I go into the kitchen and rummage under the sink. A tin of shoe polish only dad used rolls onto the floor. When I go to stand up, vomit fills my mouth and I dart outside the kitchen door. Leaning over the small wall, I wretch until there's nothing left.

Mum's on her hands and knees by my father's side of the bed. Grunting, she pushes the bed in my direction. Feeling like a traitor, I quietly continue filling the bags, while mum works tirelessly, scrubbing the floor until the wood is gleaming. Using the edge of the bed, she heaves herself up and looks surprised when she sees the mound of bags piled high on the bed.

"Put them in the wardrobe for now," she sighs.

With the bags tucked in the wardrobe like nothing ever happened, we go into the kitchen. I feed Chico first, keeping Meggie at a safe distance so he can eat in peace. I open the cupboard for Meggie's food, suddenly remembering I used the last can last night. She looks up at me expectantly and the lump that forms in my throat is so tight I think I might choke.

Keep it together. Keep it together.

"D'ye fancy some fish and chips?" Mum asks, throwing me for a loop. I could count on one hand the number of meals she's eaten since I arrived.

"Uh-huh," I stutter, glancing at my watch. "But I better go now, the chippy closes soon."

Mum gets up and I assume she's going back to bed but while I'm slipping my shoes on, she comes into the kitchen wearing her jacket.

Unfamiliar with navigating the country roads at night, I pull up just as the owner is preparing to lower the security grate.

"Yer fine, come in, come in," he says, giving mum a little wave.

Mum waits in the car while I order, grateful for the kind and gentle manner of the married owners, who ask about mum's wellbeing.

"I'll throw in a few extra chips for Meggie," the wife says. "That's what your dad always did."

Distracted by the scent of vinegar smothered chips wafting up from the steaming newspaper on mum's lap, I drive slowly so as not to miss the turn.

"Can ye show me the place where I might go and live?"

"Now?"

She nods just in time for me make the turn in the opposite direction.

On the advice of mum's social worker and psychiatric team, I've visited a handful of local care homes, leaving each one feeling more despondent than when I entered. All, with the exception of this one, where the care givers appeared friendly and engaging and the newer building didn't reek like the others.

I reverse into one of the dozen or so parking spots. Ahead of us, the two- story building is aglow, some rooms offering a glimpse of spritely staff aiding ailing residents.

"Whit's that next door?" mum asks.

"It's a primary school."

"So, if I was to come and li… be here, I'd hear the wee ones on the playground?"

I nod and put a chip in my mouth I can barely swallow.

With the lantern at the base of the bridge lighting the way, I hold the gate open for mum. From the nearby woods, the sound of hooting owls makes me think of my father.

"In Greek mythology," dad would tell me more than once, "the owl signifies wisdom and reason. That's probably why ye like them."

"Wisdom and reason," I utter.

"Give me a wee hand getting doon the path," mum says, bringing me back to the present. Halfway down she stops. "Is that dad's flowers?"

I pluck two white lilies from the pale funeral palette, the passing of time evident from their browning edges. I take mum's arm, making sure to avoid the loose cobblestones. At the water's edge, she sways a little and I move her a few steps back. Her hand grips my arm as she gazes up at the bridge.

"I'll never forget the first time I saw this."

Neither of my parents ever learned to drive, so when it came time for the move from England to Scotland, they employed the services of Eamon, a longtime friend who offered to drive the moving van, complete with Tini, the dog.

"The van's stuffed to the gills," dad sighed on the phone. "Mum's hell bent on taking everything we've ever owned. I've no idea how we'll fit it all in."

"Does mum know how big the cottage is?"

His pregnant pause told me she didn't.

After heading North all night, they arrived in the village, where the majority of the two hundred plus residents were still asleep. The sun was just starting to come up and Eamon, firmly lodged in the driver's seat, said he'd help unload the van, "After a bit of shut eye."

Liz and Tom stepped out onto the layby adjacent to the cottage and watched, bleary eyed, as Tini made his way down the dew-covered grassy knoll.

Dad stretched and inhaled the crisp air. "What do ye think, Lizzie?"

Mum turned slowly, pausing to take in the view of the church across the street, her eyes resting on the ancient headstones, visible through the black wrought iron fence.

"Quiet neighbours," dad joked.

Mum shot him a look before turning her attention to Tini.

"What do ye think of the cottage?" he asked.

"Seems awful big for just the two of us," mum replied, mistaking the grand house across the river for their new abode.

Taking mum by the shoulders, dad slowly turned her in the direction of the cottage. Mum spun around and glared at him. "*That* better not be it!"
Dad's grimace told her indeed it was their new home.

Marching towards the cottage, mum threw her arms in the air. "The windaes are boarded up! The bloody place is condemned! I cannae believe you brought me to this!"

"We'll get it all up to snuff," dad said, catching up to her. "Listen."

Mum's face softened. "The river?"

Dad nodded and held out his hand. Mum took it and followed him but before they rounded the corner to the garden, he gestured for her to stop. "I want this to be a surprise."

Mum's eyes rolled to the decrepit sandstone structure, some of which lay crumbled by her feet. "I think *this* is enough of a surprise!"

"Shut your eyes," dad urged, squeezing her hand for good measure. For the first time in three decades of marriage, mum did as he asked and allowed him to lead the way. Never one to embrace patience, she asked if she could open her eyes.

"In a wee second," dad said, positioning her in the spot that would become the focal point of countless future photographs.

Anytime mum relayed this story, she'd rest her hand on her heart. "I couldnae believe my eyes. The auld bridge was just, ye know, *there*. It had such *presence*. All ye could hear was the water, trickling its way under the arches. It literally took my breath away."

Hand in hand, Liz and Tom stepped precariously over jagged rocks, clods of mud and grassy mounds, to the river's edge, where Tini lapped up the water.

"Fancy a wee dip?" Dad teased as mum raised her eyes in wonder to the bridge.

"So, ye like it then?"

Mum nodded. "Aye, but we're no living oot here, we're living in there," she said pointing to the cottage.

"Don't worry Lizzie," dad assured her. "I won't let ye down."

Weariness washed over mum and she asked dad to retrieve the box with the tea kettle. "I'm gasping for a wee cuppa. And when Eamon wakes up, first thing oot the van is the settee." Dad gave her a sheepish look.

"Whit noo?"

"It might be a wee while before we can use the living room."

Mum's hands went to her hips as she lowered her head in anticipation of dad's explanation.

"The rain got in through, ehm, a wee spot in the roof."

"When ye say a *wee spot*, d'ye mean a *giant gaping hole*?"

"The weight of the water took its toll on the ceiling, causing it to, ehm, cave in."

Mum shook her head. "And the kitchen? Can we at least use the kitchen?"

Dad nodded enthusiastically, his fingers crossed behind his back, hoping there'd be no burst pipes when he turned on the water.

"Well then," mum sighed, "considering the shock you've given me, I think the least you can do is take me inside this, this, whatever this is, and make me a wee cuppa tea."

"Tea? That's all ye want?"

"Aye, tea," she retorted.

"Phew," dad said, swiping his hand across his forehead in an exaggerated fashion. "I thought ye were going to ask me to carry ye over the threshold!"

"This wee place has been good to us," mum says, as I hand her a lily. She presses it to her chest and closes her eyes. I wait for her to finish praying. When she opens her eyes, she gestures, *ready?*

In unison, we toss the lilies into the water.

She swallows hard before she says, "Thank you, Tom."

"Love you, dad," I whisper, watching the lilies as they separate and float away.

THE INN

The wind's blowing a hoolie and the cottage is shrouded in darkness when I pull the rental car into the layby. Thanks to several delays, Will and I have been travelling for over seventeen hours so when he asks, in a huffy tone, why I didn't, "Have someone leave the light on," I ignore him.

Using a sliver of light from the lantern at the base of the bridge, Will wastes no time getting us inside. After dragging in the luggage, he moves through the cottage, switching on every light, ending in the living room, where the urn containing my father's ashes sits on the hearth. I chide myself for leaving the urn in plain sight, even though nobody has been in the cottage since I left two months before. I keep an eye on Will, hoping he won't ask about it.

"How *long* are we staying?"

"I've told you umpteen times. Five days."

Seemingly unfazed by my agitated tone, Will reaches for a small toy car on the mantle.

"Granda kept this?"

"Not just that one. Look." I point to the shelf on the other side of the room. Feeling guilty from snapping at him one too many times, I ask if he remembers giving the cars to my father.

"I remember every time," he says, quietly. "I'd save it 'til we got to the airport."

"And when you pulled the car out of your pocket, granda would act surprised and say-" I gesture for Will to join me and in unison, we say,

"No, no son that's yours, you keep it."

Will laughs his lovely laugh. "I'd slip the car in his jacket pocket and he'd act like nothing happened."

"Do you remember the rest?"

He nods. "Uh-huh, when he got home he'd call and say, 'You'll never guess what I found in my pocket.'" Will runs his fingers along the cars. "Can I keep them?"

"You can take them all back now."

With a mug of tea in hand, I sink into the worn leather phone chair. "Ah, that's better." I wind my oversized scarf tighter around my neck and tuck my feet under my bottom. "The heat should kick in soon."

"I hope so," Will grouses. "It's freezing in here."

Maybe if you'd listened to me and brought a coat, rests on my tongue, the best place for it. He's right though, the temperature is beyond frigid, a harsh reminder my parents are gone; one in a care home, the other in an urn.

Sorrow surges through me and I know the tears are coming and when they do, I want to be alone, but I want to ensure Will is ok, so I ask if there's anything he wants to talk about.

"No, I'm good." I don't trust his tone but he's at the age where I find myself saying less instead of more, the constant effort of not prying sometimes exhausting.

"There's no internet access so you might be better off just going to sleep."

He shrugs nonchalantly. "I'll watch tv."

"Sorry, no can do, the tv went with nana to her new place."

"Seriously, mom?"

His perfectly honed disgruntled teen act is impressive but not what I'm in the mood for right now.

"See ree is lee!" I sneer.

His eye roll has the same timing as mum's. "Are you sure there's no Wi-Fi?"

"Absolutely positive."

He looks bewildered. "What did you do last time you were here?"

"I carved messages on rocks."

Slowly, I push the bedroom door open and peer in, half expecting to see mum in the bed but it's made up, just as I left it. From the wardrobe, I grab a couple of blankets and the candlewick cover that once belonged to nana.

In the living room, I'm taken aback at the sight of Will, cradling the urn.

"This is heavy," he says, not quite understanding the magnitude of his words.

The rain's battering against the windshield.
The urn's in my lap.

My tears fall on the lid faster than I can wipe them away.

"I thought you brought granda's ashes home with you?"

"That was just a small amount that I wanted to keep any maybe..." My voice trails off as Will gently places the urn back on the hearth.

"Are you ok?" I ask.

He nods.

"Are you sure?"

"Uh-huh."

My heart races in time with my babbling speech about where to find everything, ending with,

"Got it, night mom."

"Night, love you."

"Love you too."

I close the bedroom door and stare at the bed. I'm spent, but the thought of sleeping in the bed makes me feel uneasy.

After unpacking a few clothes to sleep in, exhaustion soon wins out and I climb onto the bed. First, I lie on my mother's side, then I roll over to my father's, but that doesn't feel right either, so I wriggle to a spot in the middle. Willing my eyes to stay shut, I breathe deeply in and out, the act of which has the opposite effect of calming. Starting at one hundred, I count back in multiples of seven. When I get to two, I start counting upwards, in French, giving up when I can't recall the word for eighty.

A chill quickly winds its way through my socks as I twist open the venetian blind and the shadow cast by the lantern gently illuminates the array of flower pots that once overflowed with colour. Closing my eyes, I hear my father whistling as he opens the gate.

The only way to the bathroom is through the living room so I creep in, surprised to see Will sitting on the couch, the toy cars scattered on either side of him.

"Guess you can't sleep either?"

His shoulders heave. He sniffs and wipes his eyes. I sit next to him on the couch and reach my arm around his ever-expanding shoulders. "It's ok, Just let it all out."

If only to ground myself, I tighten my grip on his shoulder.

"It's too sad being here without them."

I squeeze harder.

"I don't want to stay here, mom. And I'm sorry I never got it."

"What do you mean?"

He pulls away from me and looks at the carpet. "When you came home after granda… died." He pauses. "I knew you were sad and I was too, but I just didn't get it." He motions to the urn. "Not like now."

I swallow hard before speaking. "Listen, I know this is a lot for you to take in and I'm sorry. I didn't think it through but I honestly didn't think it would feel this way."

He shrugs.

"But listen." I keep my tone positive. "Everything will be ok. We'll see nana in her new place tomorrow and…"

He stands, his height still a surprise to me. "I *don't* want to stay here."

I get up and reach my hands up to rest on his shoulders.

"Nor do I, but it's really late and there's nowhere else for us to go. Let's try and get some sleep and we'll figure something out tomorrow, ok?" I feel some of the tension release from his shoulders.

Will gathers up the toy cars and places them on the hearth, next to the urn. He lies on the couch and his legs dangle over the edge while he wraps the blankets around him.

"The last time you were here you fit on there. Try and get some sleep, ok?"

My stomach churns at the thought of a long sleepless night in the place where my father died. "You know what, it's too cold in the bedroom, I'm sleeping out here."

I wrap myself in the soft candlewick cover and use my scarf as a makeshift pillow, then I reach up and turn off the lamp. The cottage falls silent and I shut my eyes.

"Mom?"

"What?"

"It's only seven o'clock at home."

"Yes, but it's midnight here," I say in a mock stern voice. "Now. Go. To. Sleep!"

I'm awake at the crack of dawn, leaving Will to sleep while I enjoy my first cup of tea perched on the wall outside the kitchen door, thankful I remembered to buy milk at the airport Tesco.

Moving around the garden, I pull weeds, feeling melancholy, knowing the garden will never again look as majestic as it did when dad worked his magic.

The shop bell jingles when I open the door, causing Agnes to look up from her magazine. "Oh Karen, it's yerself," she burrs.

"Hi Agnes, nice to see you."

"When did ye arrive?" She bustles past the display shelves, the skirt on her apron narrowly catching the edge of a small table laden with locally made confectionary.

"Only last night."

She glances outside. "Is yer husband with ye?"

"No, but my son is."

"Oh, that's good. How old is he now?"

"Fifteen."

"Och, time flies! I remember the first time ye brought him over, he was just a bairn, disnae seem that long ago. Are ye staying at the cottage?"

"We stayed there last night but Will had a bit of a hard time. I can't lie, I did too. It just didn't feel... right."

"That's understandable. After we lost my father, my sister never laid foot in the flat ever again. Made it hard on me having to take care of everything, but what could I do? Loss brings out the best *and* the worst in people."

"Isn't that the truth?"

Agnes picks up a slab of tablet, tears open the wrapper and snaps off a generous piece she hands to me.

"Oooh, thank you." The sweet concoction melts on my tongue.

"Made by yours truly." Her face lights up in question.

"It's delicious. I'll take two, thanks."

"What about the inn?"

"The what?"

"The inn, what about staying there?"

"Is it open?"

"Aye, George was just in, said they're quiet at the moment."

"George?"

"The innkeeper, have you no met him?"

"I might have met him at dad's funeral but it was all a bit of a blur."

"They were awful fond of yer daddy, och we all were. Every morning without fail Tom would come in for his rolls and two newspapers. I'd kid him about the posh paper and he'd laugh and say 'just trying to keep up Agnes.' Wee Meggie would sit outside waiting for him, good as gold, never had to be tied up or anything." With her arms barely crossing her ample bosom, Agnes continues.

"What happened to Meggie and the wee cat? I dinnae ken his name."

"Chico." I smile when I say his name. "He went to a farm in Perth and Meggie went to Maybole with a lovely couple she managed to cast under her spell within five minutes of meeting her."

"That sounds like Meggie!" She chuckles. "Ye must bring your son in, I'd love to see him. And tell yer mammy I miss seeing her. She was always good for a blether."

"I'll do that but first I better buy something for breakfast."

"Och, teenage boys, there's no end to their hunger, is there?"

I cross the street by the bus stop and return the wave of a couple I don't recognize. The door to the bar at the inn is locked so I walk around to the side entrance and try the handle but it won't budge, so I give up and walk away, turning when I hear, "Karen?"

"George?" I say, walking back towards the inn. I take his outstretched hand and tell him I just came from the shop.

"Aye, Agnes just phoned to let me know you'd be stopping by."

Of course she did!

"When do you want to check in?" Just like my father, straight to the point.

"You have rooms available?"

"Aye, all four of them, you can take your pick."

"How about later today?"

"That's fine. Do you have a phone?"

"My cell doesn't work here and the house phone is disconnected."

"No problem, just chap the door next to the main door, that's where we live. And listen, I just want to say, I'm sorry about your father. I saw him more or less every day. It won't come as a surprise to hear he was quite partial to a pint of Guinness."

"I'm not sure what he enjoyed more," I laugh. "Guinness or whisky."

"Equal contenders," he smiles, pushing his glasses farther up his nose. "I'm a red wine man myself. Anyway, come up when you're ready, you'll be fine here, we'll take good care of you."

Will's stretch reaches the kitchen ceiling and, hungrily, he eyes the eggs and pack of link sausages I can't wait to sink my teeth into.

"Here," I say, tossing a slab of tablet in his direction. "That'll keep you going for now."

With the prospect of food, Will is much more himself but when I share the news about the inn, he really perks up.

Will is beside himself when George jots down the all-important Wi-Fi password. George winks in my direction before turning to Will.

"It's just a shame we only get internet access at the weekend."

Will's jaw drops.

"I'm just kidding," George chuckles. "Google away!"

Consciously making as much noise as possible, I move around the spacious, well- appointed room, hoping to rouse Will awake. When he doesn't stir, I scribble a note telling him to meet me at the cottage. There's an entire lifetime to be cleaned out and I don't relish the thought of doing it alone.

Downstairs, George catches me on my way out.

"Morning."

"Good morning, George."

"Did you sleep well?"

I nod in response. "Like a log!"

Are you not having breakfast?"

"Breakfast?"

"Aye ye know, the first meal of the day, typically with eggs and bacon or in this case a wee bit of black pudding."

My expression tells him I'm not a big black pudding fan, making him tut.

"Don't worry, we won't throw you out for not eating it, follow me."

In a room off to the side of the dining room, one of a handful of tables is set for two.

"I don't think we'll be seeing Will anytime soon," I say, unfolding the cloth napkin and placing it in my lap.

George heads for the kitchen as a woman about mum's age appears from the main dining area. Smiling warmly, she holds out her hand.

"Hi Karen, I'm Alice, George's wife."

I stand and shake her hand. "It's really nice to meet you."

"I have to say your resemblance to your mother is uncanny. Are you and your son comfortable? Is there anything you need?"

"No, we're fine thanks. The room is lovely, so spacious and I've already eaten most of the shortbread."

"It's a popular one. I'm glad you're here with us. Hopefully this visit will be less... arduous."

I nod in acknowledgement.

"I heard Will was happy we've heard of the internet."

I laugh. "Typical teenager, constantly connected. Oh, speak of the devil."

Sleep is plastered across Will's fair complexion and the blond peaks of his hair suggest an empty bottle of hair gel but he still manages a smile in Alice's direction.

"Hello young man, I'm Alice." Her hand lingers in his.

"Hi Alice, nice to meet you. I'm Will."

"You're tall and handsome, like your granda." She motions for Will to sit.

"Fiona will take your order in a wee minute. I would recommend the full Scottish breakfast."

From behind Alice, a chocolate Labrador ambles in our direction.

"Ah, here comes Rex," she says, bending to pat the dog as he passes her. In true dog form, Rex laps up every ounce of attention before finding a spot under the table.

George returns. "Rex, are you making friends with Will in the hopes he'll feed you?"

Rex's tail whips the tartan carpet. George's expression turns deadly serious.

"Will, did you hear the news?"

Will eyes him dubiously.

"You blew up the internet!"

It takes Will a second to register the joke. Alice swipes George's arm.

"George, leave the boy alone. Right, well I'll leave you to it, let us know if you need anything. Please tell your mum I'm asking for her. I miss seeing her out and about."

With full tummies, Will and I make our way down Main Street, stopping to chat to many of the inhabitants, all of whom know Will by name and speak fondly of my parents. With every step, I think of my father and how much I miss laughing with him over silly stuff before delving into deep discussions about world events, when he'd voice his opinion I rarely agreed with.

In the cottage I light a few candles and open the windows to air out the place. I wipe down the kitchen counters and when I open the side door, Will's making his way up the path. I open my mouth to warn him to be careful on the loose cobbles, quickly reminding myself he's fifteen.

We sit on the wall outside the kitchen door and I turn my face to the sun, listening as the rocks Will skips land on the glass like surface. He sighs a heavy sigh.

"Why can't we keep this place?"

I mirror his sigh. "Trust me, I've racked my brain trying to figure out a way to keep it but we need the money to take care of nana in her new place."

"I thought nana and granda wanted you to have the cottage?"

"That was their wish but sadly granda died before the seven-year time period had passed, so the things he put in place became void."

"So, if granda lived longer we'd be all set?"

I nod in response.

"Are you still sad, mom?"

I look at his open face, his father's eyes, my father's nose. My heart soars at the beautiful combination.

"It comes and goes but everyone says it gets easier as time goes by."

Later that day, while I'm engrossed in a photo album of our first family holiday to the Costa Brava, I hear the thrum of an engine and when I look out the side window, Will is mowing the lawn.

THE NEW OWNERS

I'm slathering my toast in Drambuie marmalade when George comes into the dining nook.

"Morning, Karen."

"Craig should bottle this and sell it," I remark as George takes a seat on the banquet opposite, as he's wont to do when I'm the only guest.

"It's good stuff isn't it?"

"Oh aye, yer boy's the business," I reply in my broadest Scottish lilt. "Where's Alice?"

"She's out walking. She left me a list of jobs but first, coffee." He sips the freshly brewed coffee, the smell of which fills the small nook.

"How's your mum?"

I'm chewing a chunk of toast so I tilt my hand from side to side.

"So-so?"

I nod and take a gulp of tea to wash down the toast.

"How'd it go yesterday?"

"It went well, the lawyer met us at the care home, the papers got signed and... it's done." More tea to loosen the tightness in my throat.

"The lads came in last night looking for you."

"What lads?"

"The new owners."

"They were here?"

"Aye, they heard you were staying here but Alice told them you were still up visiting your mum."

"Oh," I utter, so many questions forming. "What are they like?"

"They're young and they've a good sense of humour. Had us in stitches telling us about the disaster in the living room."

I look at him in question as he repositions his body, reminding me of my father, how his posture would change before sharing an amusing anecdote.

"They were poking about the ceiling, something about wanting to install recessed lights, you know, getting an idea of what could be changed. All of a sudden, the entire ceiling came tumbling down on top of them!"

My mouth drops open. I toss the napkin on the table and go to get up.

"Where are you going?"

"I have to go down there!" A vision of my father wagging his finger from above.

I'm going! I'm going!

"Finish your breakfast first, it's still early."

The rental car sits solo in the car park, blanketed in a light smattering of snow, the windshield covered in ice

I can't be bothered to scrape, so I zip up my coat and start walking.

At the end of the street I decide to take the long way so I head for the path that climbs high above the village. I pass the bowling green and the village hall, pausing to scan the notice board, intrigued by the poster advertising Tai Chai classes.

Up ahead, a steady stream of work vans and lorries stop outside the shop, no doubt grabbing food to go, my favourite being lorne sausage, which happens to be square and best enjoyed in a crusty roll.

A woman I don't recognize steps out of the mobile bank van and waves. I wave back and from across the street she shouts, "How's yer mammy?"

"Fine," I nod.

"Tell her I'm asking for her."

The wooden gate groans a morning yawn when I push the weight of my body against it to shove the snow out of the way. Trudging up the path, I wind my scarf around my head and pull it up over my mouth but the chill still finds its way in.

At the top, I stop to take a breath, appreciating the view of the entire village, bordered on either side by fields of frost glistening against the vivid blue sky. The crisp air is mixed with the smell of coal and peat rising up through the chimney pots and I imagine children being roused awake for school, pleas of protest, wanting nothing more than to slip back under the blankets with a hot water bottle.

Several devoted dog owners pass, the hour too early for nothing more than mumbles about how chilly the weather is. My father's voice rings in my ears,

Ye canny beat blue sky wi a wee nip of frost in the air.

The steep incline at the end of the path forces me to slow my gait, allowing time to take in the church and the long limbs of the cemetery surrounding it. Back on level ground, I follow the curve of the stone wall, crossing the road after the bend.

Puffs of smoke billow from the rear of the cottage my friend Marie renamed Fairy Glen and just as I'm about to unlatch the gate, a young man appears, taking me by surprise.

"Karen," he says, more statement than question. He opens the gate and extends his hand, smiling. "Martyn."

"Hi, Martyn," I say, shaking his hand.

"Your hands are freezin!"

"I wanted to come and apologize about the ceiling. George just told me what happened."
I'm expecting some sort of recourse but instead he shakes his head dismissively.

"Don't worry about it," he says, with a shrug of his slender shoulders. "We're planning on making a few changes anyway."

His easy manner and lack of concern makes me want to hug him.

"Come and have a cup of tea with us."

I follow Martyn into the back garden, where another young man is fanning the flames that shoot beyond the roof line.

"Chris, this is Karen."

Chris is taller than Martyn, equally as handsome and lean, with dark hair, some of which rests over one eye. My first impression is that he's shy, but he looks me in the eye when he says, "Nice to meet you, Karen," his Glaswegian accent giving my name two syllables.

"You have chickens!" I shriek.

"We have a pig as well," Martyn says.

"You do not!"

"Do too," he replies in an exaggerated American accent. "Her name's Whoopie."

"What do you take in your tea?" Chris asks.

"Just milk, thanks." I turn to Martyn. "Nice fire."

"Aye ,we're burning the-"

"Let me guess, remnants of the ceiling?"

"You guessed it," Martyn laughs a deep laugh that I join him in. I warm my hands by the fire while Martyn shoos the chickens out of the way.

"How did you know who I was?"

The sun catches flecks of his reddish hair and he flashes a toothy grin. "George and Alice described you to a T."

We fall into an easy conversation, quickly establishing Glasgow as our birth place.

We talk about the cottage, it's history and how my parents found it. When Martyn gazes up at the bridge, it's obvious he's already smitten.

There's a knock from the kitchen window and when I look up, Chris waves. I do the same, thinking how natural it is to see him doing something I've done so many times before.

Chris returns with three mugs of tea on a tray, a jug of milk and a plate of Tunnocks tea cakes.

My kinda people!

Chris puts down the tray and passes a mug with perfectly proportioned ratio of milk to tea.

"Does that look ok?" He motions to the china jug. "There's more milk if you need it."

"This is perfect, thank you," I say, raising the mug to my mouth.

"Chris!" Martyn exclaims.

"What?" asks Chris, eyes full of innocence.

"Look at the mug you gave Karen!"

I twist the mug and emblazoned in huge letters are the words, I LOVE COCK.

I flutter my eyelashes and purr, "Secrets out, y'all!"

Martyn spits out his tea, and we crack up laughing.

With the ice well and truly broken, Martyn and I continue talking ten to the dozen, questions and answers tumbling together as Chris continues to tend to the fire, pausing to ask, "Do you mind if I let the dogs out?"

"Chickens, Tunnocks tea cakes *and* dogs? I'm never leaving!"

Daisy, a Dalmatian, and Gloria, a Bassett Hound with the longest ears I've ever seen, come bounding around the corner. They sniff my boots before tearing off in pursuit of something more interesting.

"Come and meet our pig," Martyn offers.

Whoopie has her snout to the ground, but when Martyn coos her name she looks up, keeping her eyes on him as he speaks softly to her. Pecking chickens roam in close proximity, clearly no strangers to Whoopie's presence.

"My dad would have loved... " My voice trails off.

Martyn looks at me. "We heard you were upset the night before we signed the papers."

"News travels fast around here," I say. "This year has been really difficult, and knowing I'd never be able to come here again felt pretty devastating."

"Well, you're always welcome," Martyn says, his tone lighter. "Right Whoopie? Tell Karen she can come and visit anytime."

Whoopie lets out a loud snort.

I smile at Martyn. "That means a lot, thank you. By the way, how bad is the ceiling?"

He feigns a look of confusion. "Ceiling? What ceiling?"

The living room looks like a construction site, with dust and debris everywhere.

"You should be wearing masks," I scold, looking up at the exposed rafters.
"I'm so sorry, I had no idea."

"We'll get it sorted," Martyn says. "Besides, we need something to keep the fire going."

I step over piles of insulation and plasterboard. "This is exactly what happened right before my mum and dad bought this place."

Martyn and Chris exchange a look.

"Eerie, right?"

They nod.

Chris says, "We heard your mum's in a nursing home?"

"Uh-huh, not far from here."

"How is she?" Martyn asks.

"She has dementia. Some days are better than others."

He pulls a sad face, mouths, "Sorry."

"She's in good hands. I'm heading up there now."

"Will you be at the inn later?" Chris asks.

"Yeah, I usually get back from seeing mum around seven."

"That's that sorted then," Martyn clasps his hands together. "We'll see you in the bar."

I raise my eyes to the ceiling. "Guess the bevvies are on me!"

DOUGAL

Gloria's velvety smooth ears are splayed across my lap and with the glow and warmth emanating from the coal fire it's clear she's here to stay. The newest addition to Martyn and Chris's menagerie purrs at the back of my head and I reach my hand around to scratch his tiny kitten neck.

In the two years since Martyn and Chris moved into the cottage, they've been busy making all sorts of changes, including the addition of a bedroom they insisted I use during this unexpected visit, after mum was admitted to hospital, where she remained for several weeks before finally being discharged.

Along with running their tea shop in Glasgow, Martyn and Chris have become regular visitors at mum's place, keeping her spirits up with plenty of treats and Glasgow patter.

Martyn bursts through the front door, his cheeks ruddy, his rugby shirt rumpled from tending to the animals that live outside. He blows air into his cupped hands and rubs them briskly together.

"Are you going back up to see your mum?"

I shake my head. "I think I'll give tonight a miss. Now that she's back in familiar territory, she seems exhausted, poor thing."

"Oh good," he grins. "I mean good that you're not going out again. Do you fancy going for a wee run?"

In Scotland, a wee run doesn't mean donning your sneakers, it means going for a drive.

"Aye, sure," I say, my language worlds colliding. Gloria lazily opens one eye but promptly falls back asleep after I move her to the other side of the couch.

"We're going to pick up a pig."

"A pig?"

"Caroline has one that needs a new home."

Caroline is an Irish woman with an infectious laugh, an adorable son and a penchant for animals in need. She lives deep in the countryside, which means a scenic drive, something I'm always up for.

Under the small porch outside the front door, I try not to topple over whilst slipping on my wellies, still covered in mud from yesterday's tromp through the fields. Martyn is outside the gate, pacing up and down, no doubt excited about the prospect of another pig, since Whoopie is no longer.

Standing by the passenger door of the rental car, Martyn gives me a questioning look.

"Nononononono," I sing, the penny dropping. "We are NOT using the rental car to transport a pig!"

With a sheepish look, he says, "I've had a few pints of Guinness."

Chris appears, wiping his hands on a rag. "Who's driving?"

"Obviously me," I say, sticking my tongue out at Martyn.

We pile into Martyn's car and I make the necessary adjustments to the seat and mirrors, then before pulling out I make a mental note of what side of the road I need to be on!

The March air holds the promise of a pleasant spring evening and with the radio blasting, we sing along to songs I danced to in discos, at a time when Martyn and Chris were still in nappies.

Martyn gets out and unlatches the heavy metal gate, closing it after I drive through. Caroline leads us to the back of the expansive property, littered with animals of every description and views as far as the eye can see.

In the shed, the pig has its head buried deep in a bucket of slop, the smell of which turns my stomach. When the pig finally looks up, Chris lets out a little sigh of contentment.

"Aw, look at that wee face."

"His name's Dougal," says Caroline.
Dougal returns his attention to the bucket, slurping up the last of his dinner.

Caroline and Martyn gently coax the pig into a wire crate and she secures the lock, while Dougal, reacting to being confined, releases a series of snorts.

"You won't be in there for long," Martyn soothes, as he and Caroline hoist the crate into the boot. I grimace when he slams the hatchback shut, surprised to hear it clicking into place.

Either due to the stress of being crated or the recent inhalation of his gourmet meal, Dougal's bowels give out before we're even out the gate. The putrid smell quickly fills the air and we roll down the windows as though our lives depended on it. In the back seat, Chris rummages through my bag, his eyes lighting up when he finds my bottle of Clinique Happy that he sprays liberally, like air freshener.

Halfway home, the sky darkens and it starts bucketing down. With a collective groan, we roll up the windows, eyes quickly watering from the combination of too much perfume and the stench of Dougal.

Before the crate is out of the car, I'm inside the cottage, lighting as many scented candles as I can find. I scrub my hands before switching on the tea kettle and no sooner do I plop on the couch, when Gloria reclaims her place on my lap.

The tea is quickly forgotten when Chris uncorks the first of several bottles of wine, enjoyed huddled around the fire, chuckling over, "Mingin Dougal," who Chris pops out to check on every hour or so. The more wine we consume, the sillier we become, ending with a game we often play where we each try and outdo the other with phrases we (in this instance) slur, in our broadest Glasgwegian accents, some of my favourites being; gaun yersel, shut yer geggy and gie-in it laldy.

For the past week, Chris has been planning a special breakfast for Easter Sunday. He's gone to great pains gathering the necessary ingredients for what will surely be a feast, after which the plan is to attend church. It all sounds perfect, as I drowsily fall into bed in the early hours, with Daisy the dalmatian's head on the pillow next to me.

The sound of the front door creaking wakes me up, as it does every morning, when Chris goes out to feed the animals. I'm about to doze off again when, from outside the bedroom window, Chris cries, "Martyn! The pig's gone!"

Daisy leaps off the bed and I get up and reach for my jumper. Pulling it over my head, Daisy's tail whips against my leg. She responds when I tell her to sit, but the second I open the bedroom door, she bolts outside, to where Chris shouts, "Martyn! Get a move on!"

Chris shoos Daisy back inside and Martyn comes out of the bedroom, rubbing his eyes. Without uttering a word, he glides past me, out the front door and through the gate. I stand in the doorway and watch as the pair of them, both in bathrobes and slippers, disappear around the bend.

In the kitchen, the dogs and cats circle my feet, purring and barking in rising decibels. In the last cabinet I open, I find their food. The cacophony only increases as I pull open drawer after drawer, in search of a can opener.

With the pets fed, I make tea, leaving it to cool while I go and make the bed. I dress quickly then open the blind, hoping for a glimpse of Dougal's sniveling snout.

I wander around the garden, go inside, make more tea, brush my teeth then sit on the couch with my book open but, after reading the same paragraph three times, I give up.

Chastising myself for not thinking of it sooner, I get in the car and drive at a snail's pace, wondering how fast a pig can walk. When I reach the outskirts of the forlorn village, I turn the car around and creep back down Main Street.

With a piping hot mug of tea, I sit on the bench outside the front door, my ears perking up when I hear Martyn's voice.

"We found him!"

With a proud air, Dougal struts between Martyn's pinstripes and Chris's polka dots. They cross the road and the words roll quickly off Martyn's tongue.

"We met a man on a bike, he stopped and said to be, 'verra verra careful, there's a wild boar on the loose!"

Showered in praise and straw, Dougal lolls in the shed while Martyn and Chris come up with ideas on how best to secure him.

With one eye on the clock, I eat much faster than usual, wishing there was more time to savour the impressive, "Full Scottish," Chris was still able to pull off.

Signifying the start of service in ten minutes, the church bell chimes, prompting a flurry of;

Is my tie straight?

Wait! I only have one earring in.

Do these shoes go with these trousers?

Are you sure this jacket's ok for church?

Don't forget money for the collection box!

With matching grins, we shuffle through the church door, swiftly taking our places on the narrow pew, just as the bell tolls and the congregation rises.

THE NEW ADDITIONS

I'm scrolling through Facebook willing myself not to click on videos of cats, when an instant message alert pops up from Martyn.

Call the house phone if you're about.

Wasting no time, I dial the fifteen-digit number I know by heart.

"Is everything ok?"

"Aye, I just wanted to tell you about our new additions."

I equate *new additions* with that of babies and knowing how keen Martyn and Chris are to be become parents, I wait with baited breath, my mind racing ahead to a church christening on a flawless summer afternoon, jugs of fruit laden Pimms cups enjoyed by the river in celebration.

Twins! They must be adopting twins!

"Sheep."

"Sheep?" I cough, my vision shattered.

"We've got two here and another two up in the field."

Two sets of twins, just not the kind I imagined!

"When you say *here*, do you mean in the garden?"

"Aye, you'll love them, they're really friendly."

Knowing the back story of just about every creature Martyn and Chris have acquired I ask where they came from.

"We saw an ad online from a farmer that was giving them away for free."

"You didn't have to pay for them?"

"Aye Karen, that's what free means in Scotland."

"Very funny. Where did they come from?"

"Down south."

"England?"

"Aye that's the term we use in Scotland for anything south of the border. You've obviously lived in America too long to remember that!"

"Oh, aren't you full of it today! How did you get them home?"

"In the car."

Of course!

I have no idea how much sheep weigh but I don't imagine they're light.

"Did they protest?"

"Aye, they had placards and everything. Seems they're quite eloquent."

"Stop it! I'm just trying to establish-"

In a posh voice he says, "I'm just trying to establish…"

"Ok I'll shut up so you can tell me what happened."

"The farmer wanted to part with six sheep and he seemed a bit surprised when we said we'd take all of them. He asked how we'd move them and I pointed to the car. 'No way, mate,' he kept saying."

I'm about to cut in when Martyn says, "Did you know you cannae transport sheep in a car?"

"I do now!"

"Apparently, you need a licence, some EU law that came into effect a few years ago. Obviously, we had nothing of the sort so Chris and I were just standing there looking at each other, like, we drove four hours for *this*?"

"So how did you get them home?"

"I'm getting there, hang on a minute, somebody's at the door."

No sooner have I filled my tea kettle when Martyn says, "That's me back, where was I?"

"You were at the front door."

He chuckles. "That was Isobel with tickets for the ceilidh next month."

"Oh, where's that being held?"

"At the wee community hall. Shame you won't be here for it."

"I'd need a refresher course on the Eightsome Reel, but you were saying-"

"Aye, so the farmer started rattling on about the EU ruling and how mad all the health and safety stuff is but once we got talking he calmed down a wee bit."

"That's you Martyn, gift of the gab."

"Aye you can talk. Anyway, we made it clear the only way we could take them was in the car, it's no as if we just live down the street but we reassured him we'd take good care of them, you know what we're like when it comes to animals."

"What'd he say to that?"

"He said he'd make himself *scarce*. That way he wouldn't see us taking them."

"How on earth did you get the sheep in the car?"

"One at a time. They're heavy but docile so it was quite easy getting them in. The others just waited as if they knew they were getting a good deal."

"A good deal?"

"Aye well you can imagine where their next stop was."

"Poor wee souls," I utter.

"Anyway, we didnae waste any time, you know, just in case somebody passed on the road but it was quiet."

"You managed to fit six sheep in your car?"

"Aye, they were all facing forward but once we were on the road, they all turned at the same time and ended up looking out the back window."

It takes a minute for me to stop laughing.

"Hang on, you said you had two in the garden and two in the field. What happened to the other two?"

"Soon into the journey we realized the sheep were too crammed and probably uncomfortable so while we were discussing what to do, we came across another farm. That farmer looked surprised to see we had sheep in the car and I asked if he'd be interested in taking a few of them off our hands so he asked how much?"

"But you got them for free!"

Ignoring my comment, he continues. "He offered us eighty quid for two of them and he even made us a cup of tea!"

"So, you brought four home?"

"Aye but four was too many in the garden so when we were talking to the shepherd in the pub the other night-"

"The shepherd?"

"Aye, Duncan, he's a lovely man, knew your dad well. Speaks very highly of Tom."

"Ah, yes, Duncan."

"He said we keep could two up in the field as long as we kept an eye on them."

"How many sheep are in the field?"

"I don't know, mibbe a hundred or so."

"Then how will you know which ones are yours?"

"Och, I'll remember them."

A month later, after what can only be described as a dizzying night at the cottage, Martyn and I head out for a walk to clear our heads. Traffic on the country road is sparse but at the sight of oncoming vehicles, we stop on the grassy verge, with me at one point losing my footing on the uneven surface, the sight of which propels Martyn into hysterics.

"Are you still drunk?"

I rub my temples, vowing never to drink so much ever again.

"This walk will help," he says. "Especially on such a nice night when it won't get dark until after ten."

"Sky for miles," I sigh in contentment. "I love it."

"Do you think you'll ever move back to Scotland?"

"Who knows," I shrug.

"Your mum would love that wouldn't she? She was in good form when we visited last week, her patter's brilliant, Glesga lassie through and through."

"She is that," I laugh.

"It's a shame Will couldn't come with you."

"He was adamant he didn't want to miss sailing camp and now he's driving that's all he wants to do, but he'll come next time."

"Be good to see him again and let him see the changes we've made to the cottage."

Fueled by chips and pickled onions, we walk at a decent clip on the way back. We've been out for hours and I'm more than ready to free my feet from the wellies but when we reach the bridge Martyn asks if I want to go up to the field and see his sheep.

We continue walking, passing the church and the cemetery before trudging up the steep hill. After the entrance to the castle, the road levels, opening to fields on either side, one scattered with sheep.

"That's us," Martyn says, slipping through a gap in the fence I have to suck everything in, in order to squeeze through.

Moving with purpose, he tromps halfway across the field, stopping by a huge plane tree, under which sit two sheep.

"This is them," he says, bending to pat the sheep.

"Are you pulling my leg?"

"Naw," he says shaking his head. "This is definitely them. Aren't they lovely?"

On the way back down the hill, a mischievous grin spreads over Martyn's sunburned face. "Pub?"

"No way! Not after last night!"

"Come on, you're on holiday."

Rounding the bend, we see Chris outside, watering the flowers in the window boxes.

"Chris," Martyn shouts. "Meet us in the pub."

I give Martyn a look. "Just one. That's *all* I'm having."

Martyn links his arm through mine. "Aye, right, we'll see about that!"

Printed in Great Britain
by Amazon